PHILATELIC TERMS ILLUSTRATED

Compiled by Russell Bennett
and James Watson

SECOND EDITION

*By Appointment to Her Majesty The Queen,
Stanley Gibbons Ltd., London,
Philatelists*

**Stanley Gibbons Publications Ltd,
391 Strand, London WC2R 0LX**

A1
A2
A3
A4
POSTAGE
TWO PENCE
A5
REPUBLIQUE DU CONGO
150F
POSTE AERIENNE
L'ENFANT AUX CERISES · JOHN RUSSELL (1745-1806)
A6
LATVIJA
A7
A8
A9
POSTAGE ONE SHILLING
CAPE OF GOOD HOPE
A10
DEUTSCHE BUNDESPOST
30 + 15
FÜR DIE JUGEND 1970
A11
COOK ISLANDS
30c
A12
VICTORIA
HALF-PENNY
A13
PEARS' SOAP.
Fry's PURE CONCENTRATED Cocoa
BONNINGTON'S IRISH MOSS
A14
A15
A16

A17

A18

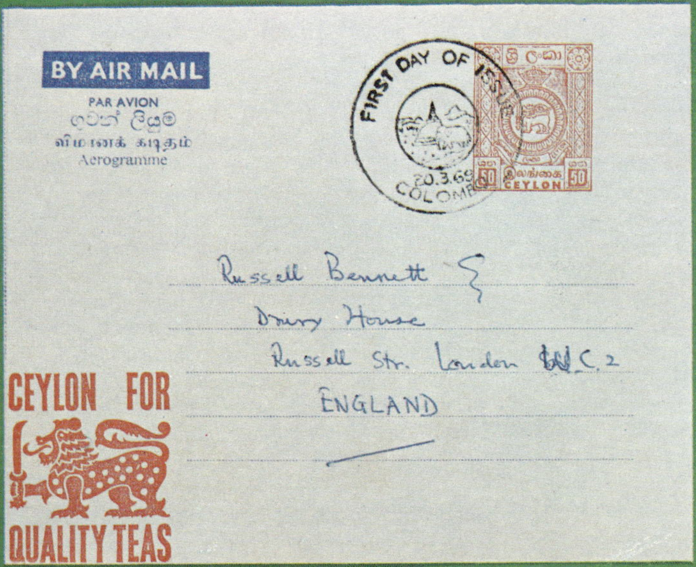

A19

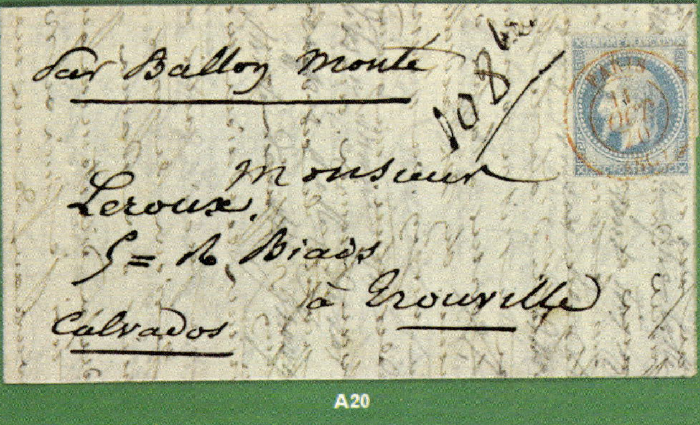

A20

This illustrated dictionary of philatelic terms has been compiled from the famous Stanley Gibbons reference collection which has been displayed to many philatelic societies in Great Britain. Acknowledgment is also given to the Glossary of Philatelic Terms published by the Philatelic Congress of Great Britain.

Abnormal. Stamps of Great Britain, 1862–80, printed from certain plates, or in certain colours from certain plates, are known as 'Abnormals' because they were not normally issued. Only five sheets of these stamps were prepared for registration at Somerset House. Examples now in collectors' hands are from those sheets which it is thought were later put into Post Office stock.
Illustration: A1, the 9d. from Plate 5.

Acknowledgment of Receipt. A special stamp is issued in some countries to denote the fee paid for the acknowledgment of receipt of a postal item. Usually the initials 'A.R.' are incorporated in the design or overprinted on an ordinary postage stamp, those letters standing for 'Aviso de Recepcion' (advice of receipt).
Illustrations: A2–4, Colombia (Antioquia), Montenegro, Panama.

Adhesive. Implies a stamp intended to be affixed to letters or postal packets, etc., by means of gum or other adhesive substance, as distinguished from one embossed or printed direct upon an envelope, card or other form of stationery.
Illustrations: A5–13, a selection of various shapes and styles of adhesives from the 1840 2d. Blue to modern times, including the world's smallest stamp from Colombia (Bolivar), A9.

Marginal advertising from South Africa

Advertisements on Stamps. In Great Britain the idea of advertising on the backs of postage stamps never went beyond the experimental stage, but in New Zealand stamp advertisements were actually permitted for some time, and the Queen's portrait series of 1882–97 may be found with a variety of advertisements on the backs of its stamps. Many modern Sierra Leone 'self-adhesives' have advertisements printed on the backing paper. 'Adson' is the term coined to describe all these issues.
Illustrations: A14–16, New Zealand 1882–97.

Air Mail. Implies the carriage of letters and packets by some form of aerial transport. In many countries special stamps are provided for such mail and additional postal rates are usually charged. The only special stamps used in Great Britain are of a semi-official or private nature. *Illustrations: A17–18, Netherlands, Salvador.*

Aerogramme. Lightweight airletter sheets, with gummed flaps, mostly bearing a printed stamp. These are carried by air at special low rates of postage and developed from the overseas Forces Airletters used during the Second World War.
Illustration: A19.

A Christmas Airgraph

Airgraph. To speed up mail to and from British troops serving in the Middle East from 1941, the British Post Office used photography and it was possible for letters to be delivered within two weeks instead of eight weeks or more when carried by sea in the ordinary manner. A special form was provided on which the message or letter was written, together with the recipient's name and address. A photographic negative was then made, measuring five eighths by half an inch and the film was then despatched by air to the appropriate Post Office where it was developed and enlarged. The enlarged print, officially termed an 'Airgraph' was placed in a special envelope and delivered. The 'Airgraph' was not a new idea as this system for conveying messages was used during the Franco-Prussian War of 1870, during the siege of Paris. Then the films were carried by pigeons and a magic lantern was used to project the message upon a screen.

"PAR AVION"
Ship to Shore
Via Steamship Bremen and
Airplane
KATAPULTFLUG
vom
D. „BREMEN"
des Norddeutschen Lloyd
nach
BREMEN. 2.8.1929.
Mr. Monroe Moskowitz,
% Dalwick,
Cotswold, Pixham, Dorking,
London, England.
1161
VARICK ST. STA. N.Y.
JUL
4-PM
1929
5c
AIR MAIL

A21

LA UNIVERSAL
(PHILATELIC SHOP)
OREILLY 33
HABANA, CUBA.
REPUBLICA DE CUBA
SECRETARIA DE COMUNICACIONES
PRIMER VUELO
TREN AEREO
INTERNACIONAL
HABANA-MIAMI
MAYO 19-1935
PILOTOS:-O'MEARA y du-PONT.
HABANA CUBA
MAY 19
5:30PM
1935
REPUBLICA DE CUBA
ERNESTO BELLO
Care of POST MASTER
MIAMI Fla U S A

A22

QANTAS EMPIRE AIRWAYS LTD.
PARACHUTE MAIL
TO MORNINGTON ISLAND
1942
By
QANTAS
EMPIRE AIRWAYS LTD
QANTAS EMPIRE AIRWAYS LTD.
BY FLYING BOAT.
VHABG Coriolanus
COMMANDER.
Qantas Empire Airways Ltd.,
% Rev. R. Braunholz,
MORNINGTON ISLAND,
Via QUEENSLAND.
14 DAYS
SYDNEY
G.P.O. SYDNEY
R.C.S.
N.S.W.-AUST.

A23

A24

A25

A26

FROM	DATE	TIME	LAT.	LONG.

AIR PIGEON LOFT No. 1

ROYAL AIR FORCE PIGEON SERVICE.

To be taken Immediately to nearest Postal Telegraph Office.

F.S. Form 197.

A27

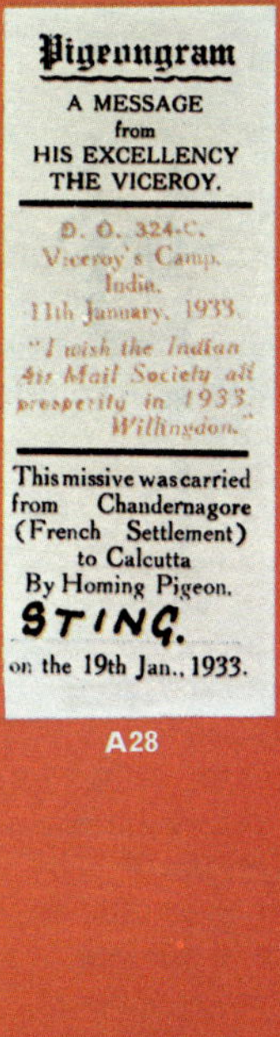

Pigeongram

A MESSAGE from HIS EXCELLENCY THE VICEROY.

D. O. 324-C.
Viceroy's Camp.
India.
11th January, 1933.

"I wish the Indian Air Mail Society all prosperity in 1933.
Willingdon."

This missive was carried from Chandernagore (French Settlement) to Calcutta By Homing Pigeon.
STING.
on the 19th Jan., 1933.

A28

A29

A30

Balloon Post. Used to denote letters officially carried by balloon, e.g. from Paris during the Franco-Prussian War, 1870–2, and from Przmysl during the First World War, 1914–18. The French description 'Ballon Monté' means that the mail-carrying balloon was manned by an aeronaut, whilst 'Ballon Non-Monté' denotes that the balloon was unmanned. *Illustration: A20.*

Catapult Mail. In 1928 the French Postal Authorities inaugurated a 'ship to shore' service in order to speed up delivery of trans-Atlantic mails. Letters specially inscribed and bearing air fee of 2s. 6d. per ½ oz. were conveyed by aeroplane catapulted from the deck of the ship about 600 miles from land, and stamps specially surcharged were used. This system was also utilised on German ships.
Illustration: A21, Cover catapulted from SS. 'Bremen' in 1929.

Glider Mail. Transmission of mails by air glider. In Cuba a service was inaugurated in 1935, in which several gliders were towed by an aeroplane. This was termed an 'Air Train' and regular air mail stamps were specially overprinted for this service.
Illustration: A22.

Parachute Mail. Messages have often been dropped by parachute. Once yearly the Qantas Empire Airways flying boat on its regular flight to Sydney, Australia, would fly low enough over Mornington Island to drop small parachute containers of Christmas parcels and letters for the Australian Inland Mission station.
Illustration: A23.

Pigeon Post. The first official pigeon post was inaugurated during the Franco-Prussian War of 1870–2, when Paris was in a state of siege. Micro-filmed messages were carried by pigeons in sealed tubes. These were then projected by magic lantern on to a screen. The Great Barrier Pigeongram Service between Auckland, New Zealand and Great Barrier Island (situated 65 miles North West) was the first to use special stamps. It was established in November 1897, but the stamps were not issued until a year later. In modern times pigeons have been used as official message-carriers by various armed forces, especially in time of war; also, other unofficial services are in use from time to time, items carried being of a 'philatelic souvenir' nature.
Illustrations: A24–26, Great Barrier Island stamps; A27, RAF Pigeongram form; A28, Pigeongram message flown in India in 1933.

Rocket Post. Many experiments have been carried out for the transmission of mail by aerial rocket, particularly in India and America. The first rocket post to be sanctioned by the Postal Authorities in Great Britain was fired on 6 June 1934 at Rottingdean, near Brighton, Sussex. Special stamps have been issued in various countries for this service, but most of them are of a private and purely speculative nature.
Illustrations: A29–30, Austria, Western Isles.

Alphabet letters 'KO–OK' on a GB $\frac{1}{2}$d. stamp of 1870

Alphabet Letters. A term used to denote the letters in the corners of the earlier issues of Great Britain; these letters are grouped into 'alphabets' corresponding to characteristic types. Also found on early stamps of Victoria (Australia).
Illustration: A31

Aniline Colour. 'Aniline' should, strictly speaking, only be applied to colours of a particular chemical origin—those derived from coal tar—but *philatelically* the term is understood to mean a peculiar quality of brightness coupled with suffusion of colour on the surface of the stamp and the colour showing through to a marked degree on the back.
Illustrations: A32–33, two 'Aniline' stamps from Brazil.

Arrow Block. A marginal arrow-shaped marking is printed on the selvedge of certain modern issues, primarily of Great Britain, to assist registration in printing and indicate convenient points of separation into panes; collected in blocks of four stamps or more.

A pair of Bantams

Black Bar

Bantams. Nickname for reduced size stamps issued by South Africa to conserve paper during the Second World War.

Black Bar. A marginal marking printed alongside the arrows on certain sheets of the first Great Britain 'phosphor' stamps to assist checking in the PO Supplies Department.

A32

A31

A33

B1

B2

B3

B4

B5

B6

B7

B8

C1

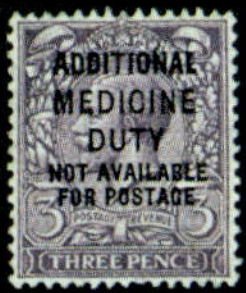

C2

C3

C4

C5

C6

C7

C8

C9

C10

C11

C12

C13

Block of Stamps. Any multiple of unsevered stamps (except where they form a complete sheet or pane) which contains at least two parallel rows of stamps in any direction.
Illustration: B1.

Bogus. A pretended stamp which is fictitious; or an actual stamp which bears the sham addition of an unauthorised surcharge or overprint. A bogus stamp is *not* a forgery, because it never officially existed.
Illustrations: B2, Bogus surcharge; B3–4, Bogus stamps; B5, Bogus perforation.

Booklet Stamps. Stamps issued bound into small books, frequently interleaved with advertisements. The first stamp booklets appeared in Luxembourg in 1895; they were introduced in Great Britain in 1904. Stamp Booklets are often made up from sheets specially printed for this purpose, with a narrow selvedge at one side of each Booklet Pane for binding. Guillotining to size frequently results in imperforate edges on stamps from booklets.
Illustration: B6, Switzerland.

Burélage. A French term used to imply a network, usually composed of wavy lines or dots. This forms the background upon which the stamp is printed, the addition of the burélage, being intended to make forgery more difficult.
Illustration: B7, Albania.

Burélé. Having a burélage incorporated in the design. Certain stamps of Queensland have a burélé band across the back.
Illustration: B8, Queensland 1879 and 1896 issues.

A Private Cachet

Cachet. A printed, embossed or (usually) handstamped inscription or device impressed on a cover to denote the special circumstances in which it has been posted (e.g. an expedition or special flight). The cachet may be *official* and applied by the Post Office, or *private* and applied independently of Post Office authority.

Cancellation. A mark of defacement of any kind applied to a stamp or item of postal stationery to prevent it being used again. It includes a postmark or postal obliteration, a pen-mark, words printed, perforated or handwritten, bars, circles and punched holes.
Illustrations: C1–5.

Cancelled. Remainders of stamps sold by certain countries to the stamp trade were overprinted 'Cancelled'. It has also been printed or written on the stamps of Great Britain and other countries instead of the word 'Specimen'.
Illustrations: C6–7.

Cancelled to Order. Generally understood to mean stamps which are postmarked or cancelled but have not actually passed through the post. A full, technical description cannot be given here, but briefly, C.T.O. stamps come either from withdrawn stocks cancelled in sheets and sold as remainders, or new issues specially postmarked or cancelled in sheets for sale at reduced rates, via the stamp trade, to collectors. 'Postmarked to Order' is also used, especially when stamps purchased at face value at the Post Office counter are postmarked by the clerk, on request.
Illustrations: C8–9, North Borneo, Czechoslovakia.

Carlist Stamps. Stamps authorised by Don Carlos and issued in certain Spanish provinces during 1873–4, the period when he assumed the title of King Carlos VII of Spain.
Illustrations: C10–11.

Centred. A perforated stamp is said to be well centred when the design is accurately positioned centrally between the four perforated edges.
Illustration: C12.

Off Centre. A term used to denote inaccurate perforation, resulting in uneven margins between the stamp design and the perforated edges. In extreme examples the perforation cuts through the design.
Illustration: C13.

Charity Stamps. Stamps which, while available for postal purposes, also acknowledge funds collected for some philanthropic object. If not available for postal purposes, such items are 'Labels', not stamps.
Illustrations: C14–21, Trinidad and Tobago, France, Peru, Surinam, Russia, Netherlands and Switzerland.

C14

C15

C16

C17

C18

C19

C20

C21

C22

C23

C24

C25

C26

C27

C28

C29

C30

C31

C32

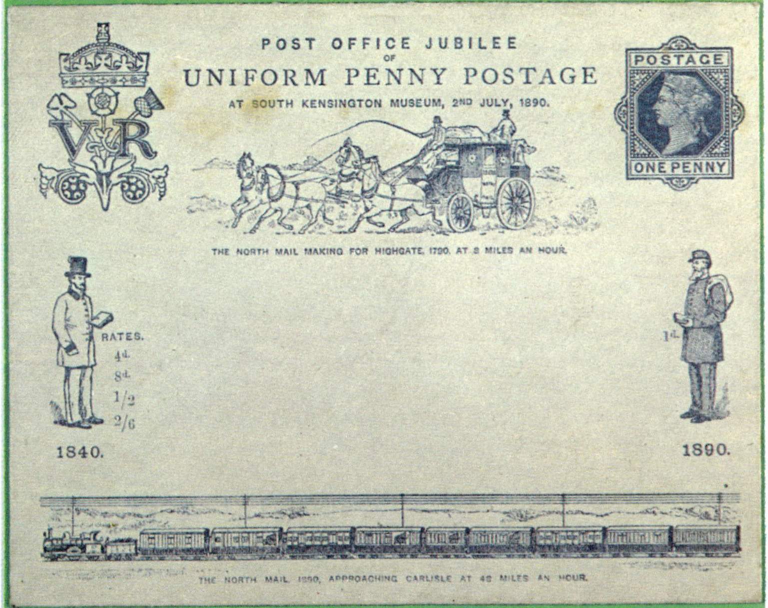

C33

Great Britain
1840
Penny Black

Belgium 'Medallions'

Cape of Good Hope
Triangular 'Woodblock'

Classic. Mainly used to describe certain stamps issued prior to 1875, but sometimes applied to more modern rarities.

Cleaned Plate. When ink clogs a printing plate after continual usage the resultant stamps are poorly printed. Stamps printed from the same plate, after cleaning, will look sharp and clean and are easily distinguishable as being from the 'Cleaned Plate'.
Illustrations: C22, Before cleaning; C23 Cleaned Plate.

Coil Stamps. Stamps issued to the public from stamp vending machines. They are specially printed and made up into coils or rolls containing hundreds of stamps, reeled sideways or lengthways, and can show consequent variations in watermark position. Frequently imperforate on parallel sides.
Illustrations: C24, Japan; C25, Coil 'join', showing two thicknesses of paper joined.

Commemorative Issues. Stamps or postal stationery issued to commemorate an event or personage. Usually in circulation for a limited period and mostly sold concurrently with the normal definitive stamps.
Illustrations: C26–32, selection of commemoratives, including (C26) the centenary of the first postage stamp; C33, envelope issued by the British Post Office to commemorate 50 years of penny postage.

Control number 'A11' on a GB King George V ½d. stamp

Condominium. A word used to describe joint rule shared by two or more powers over another territory. Examples include the Anglo-French New Hebrides Condominium and the former Anglo-Egyptian Sudan. *Illustrations: C34–35, New Hebrides stamps inscribed in English and French.*

Controls. ***Control Marks or Overprints.*** Sometimes it may happen that a stock of stamps is stolen from a post office or central store, and it becomes a matter of urgency to prevent those stamps being used for postal purposes to avoid loss of revenue. In such cases a device or inscription is overprinted on the remaining stocks of stamps and all usage of unoverprinted stamps is forbidden. These overprints may be found either printed or handstamped, or even written in manuscript, and are termed 'Control Overprints' or 'Control Marks'; they must not be confused with the Control Letters or Numbers detailed below. *Illustrations: C36, USA; C37, Persia; C38, Transvaal (Pietersburg); C39, Indian States (Nandgaon).*

Saudi Arabia 1917—corner marginal block showing control number

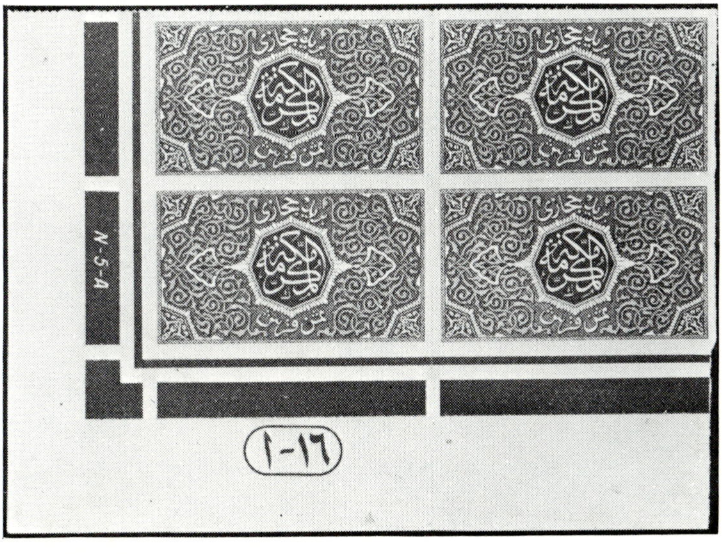

C34

C35

C36

C37

C38

C39

C40

C41

C42 C43 C44

C. G. VALSAMACHI
GALATZ
Corfú

C45

POSTAGE TWO PENCE

C46

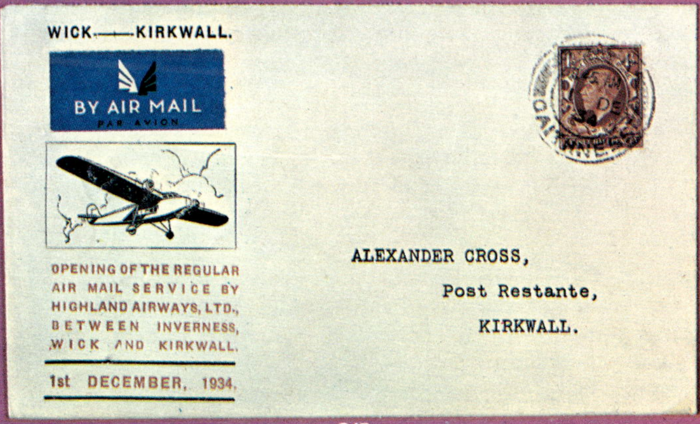
WICK——KIRKWALL.
BY AIR MAIL
PAR AVION
OPENING OF THE REGULAR
AIR MAIL SERVICE BY
HIGHLAND AIRWAYS, LTD.,
BETWEEN INVERNESS,
WICK AND KIRKWALL.
1st DECEMBER, 1934.
ALEXANDER CROSS,
Post Restante,
KIRKWALL.

C47

Control Letters and Numbers. Marginal inscriptions found on sheets of some British and other stamps. These are usually applied for the convenience of the Post Office accounting department. In the case of British issues (from 1881 until 1947) the figures refer to the year of issue and are prefixed by an index letter which denotes the half-year period (starting with 'A' for the first period of the issue).
Illustrations: C40–41.

Private Controls. These are inscriptions overprinted on stamps or printed on the backs of stamps by Private Firms, Institutions or Corporations, etc., to prevent theft from their stocks of postage stamps. They may be entirely unofficial and are really the equivalent of perforated initials.
Illustrations: C42–44.

Cover. Description applied to an envelope, wrapper or other cover of correspondence. When used stamps have been kept on their envelopes, etc., they are said to be 'on original cover'.

Combination Cover. A term used to denote covers bearing the stamps of more than one country where the stamps of each country paid the postage for a different portion of the journey.
Illustration: C45, Stamps of Greece and Austrian Italy on a cover to Corfu (the Greek stamp paid postage due on arrival).

Compound Envelope. Government postal stationery bearing more than one embossed or printed stamp.
Illustration: C46.

First Day Cover. A cover franked with a postage stamp or stamps, postmarked and sent through the post on the first day they were officially authorised for use.
Illustrations: C48, FDCs from Algeria, Israel and Hungary.

First Flight Cover. A cover which has been carried on the first mail flight between two points and which can be identified as such by either the postmarks thereon or by some special cachet or marking.
Illustration: C47, First Flight between Inverness, Wick and Kirkwall in Scotland, 1934.

Mulready Cover. William Mulready, RA, was the artist who designed the first envelopes and letter sheets issued in Great Britain in 1840 which prepaid postage. These items are always referred to by the designer's name.
Illustration: C49.

Mulready Caricature. The design of the official 'Mulready' envelope and cover was not popular. Private firms printed similar items in humorous vein to ridicule the official stationery and this eventually resulted in its discontinuance. These 'Caricatures' had no postal validity and adhesive stamps had to be attached to pay postage.
Illustration: C50.

'Patriotic' Cover. During the American Civil War large quantities of unofficial envelopes were printed and used, bearing patriotic pictures and slogans. These have come to be known as 'Patriotic' covers. *Illustration : C51.*

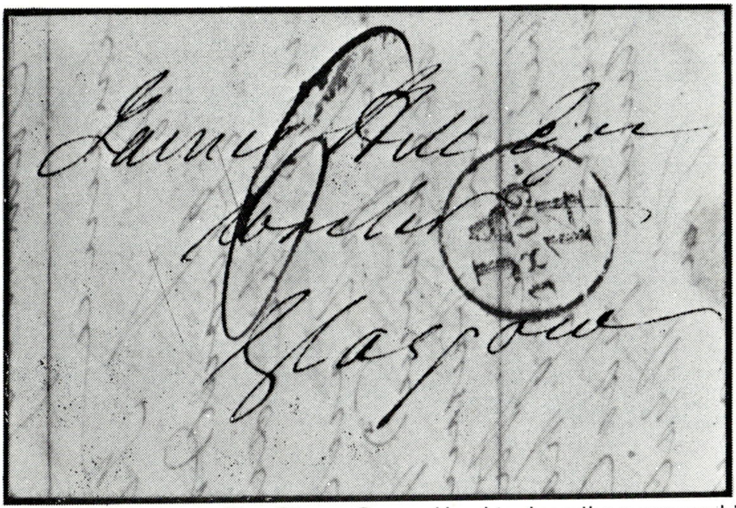

Pre-Adhesive or Pre-Stamp Cover. Used to describe a cover which has travelled through the posts before adhesive postage stamps were introduced in the country of origin.

Ship Letter. Name given to a letter which has been brought in from some comparatively inaccessible spot by sea to a port of entry in a country having a regular postal service. Generally marked 'Ship Letter', 'Loose Ship Letter' or 'Posted at Sea' and the name of the port of arrival, to facilitate charging the fee payable for the service, in addition to the ordinary postage.

الحيوانات البحرية
ANIMAUX MARINS
ALGERIE 0.75
ALGERIE 1.00
ALGERIE 0.30
ALGERIE 0.40
PREMIER JOUR
28-03-1970
ALGER
578
יום ההופעה
JOUR D'EMISSION
STAMP EDITOR,
STANLEY GIBBONS LTD.
DRURY HOUSE, RUSSELL STREET
LONDON, W.C.2. ENGLAND 42 A
ISRAEL
1870
EXPO'70
LÉGIPOSTA
MAGYAR POSTA
日本万国博覧会
BUDAPEST 4 · 1970. IV. 30.
BUDAPEST 4
4796 d
Mr. F. S. Wall
391, Strand
LONDON, W. C. 2 / ENGLAND
EXPO'70

C48

C49

C50

C51

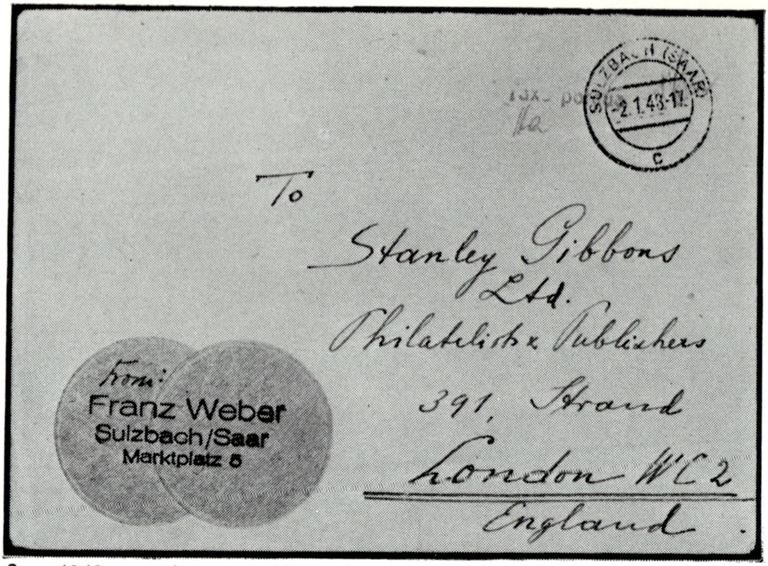

Saar 1948—no stamps available due to currency changeover

Stampless Cover. Describes a cover which has passed through the posts since the introduction of postage stamps in the country of origin, bearing some marking other than an adhesive stamp to indicate that postage has been paid. E.g. Official mail, reply-paid envelopes, hand-stamped items authorised when stamps not available, etc.

Wreck Cover. A term which denotes a cover which has been salvaged from a shipwreck and carries an official cachet to that effect. In the case of railway or aeroplane accidents the term 'Crash Cover' is more usual, although the latter are also called 'Air Accident Covers'.

Croix pattée in the Queen's diadem—GB Machin definitive

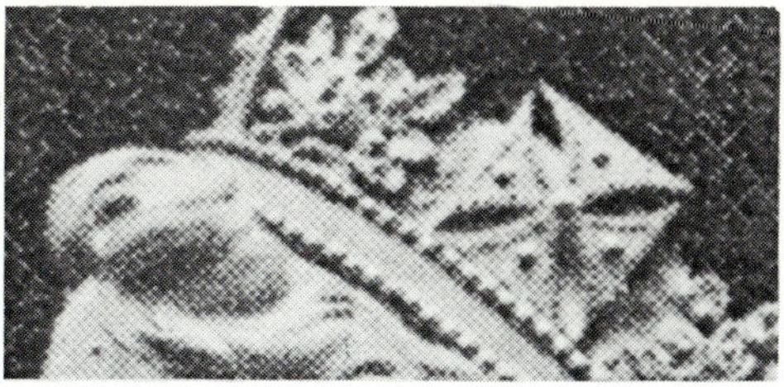

Cross. Apart from various types of cross, symbols of philanthropic societies, incorporated in the designs of stamps or overprinted on them, there are two heraldic types which are of interest to philatelists, a third type is also of interest as a paper canceller.

Croix Pattée. A cross whose arms taper towards the centre, usually with concave sides and a broad, straight end to each arm. Some early Fiji stamps have an overprint, the stop of which is in the form of a croix pattée. They can also be found in the top corners of early line-engraved Great Britain stamps. Sometimes used to describe the shape of the cancellation used on the first British stamps.
Illustrations: C52–53.

Maltese Cross. An eight-pointed cross formed by four triangles, their tops meeting in the centre, their bases indented—the top points should not overlap. This term is invariably (but erroneously) used to describe the 1840 obliteration of Great Britain.
Illustration: C54, Rodi (Rhodes).

St. Andrew's Cross. This term is used to describe the cross printed in the four vacant spaces left in panes of certain early Austrian issues, to prevent the paper being used by forgers. St. Andrew's Crosses were printed on panes in British stamp booklets for the same reason when one ½d. stamp was omitted to cover the charges made for the booklet.
Illustration: C55.

Current Numbers. These numbers were inserted in the margins of the plates of some British and early Colonial stamps to indicate the order in which the plates were made by the printers. They bear no relation to the face values of the stamps or to the territories concerned. Not to be confused with Control Numbers or Plate Numbers.
Illustration: C56.

Cylinder Numbers. Similar to plate numbers but applied to the figures in the margins of stamps printed by photogravure from rotary cylinders. A separate number appears for each different colour used in multi-coloured stamps. British stamps are usually printed in two panes, similarly numbered, but one bearing a dot after the number.
Illustrations: C57, Cylinder number below Control; C58, Multicoloured cylinder numbers.

C52

C53

C54

C55

C56

C57

C58

D1

D2

D3

D4

D5

D6

D7

D8

E1

E2

E3

E4

Dandy Roll. Wire-gauze roller which impresses the paper with its texture ('wove', 'laid', etc.) as the pulp leaves the vats. The wire or metal bits are woven or soldered on to the Dandy Roll to produce watermarks in the paper.

Definitive. A stamp specifically issued for ordinary postal needs and placed on sale for an unlimited period as opposed to commemorative, charity or provisional issues.
Illustration : D2.

Demonetised. Stamps withdrawn from circulation and deprived of any further postal validity. Demonetised stamps sold to dealers, after overprinting with some device are termed Remainders.
Illustration : D1, Switzerland, overprinted 'AUSSER KURS' ('Out of circulation').

Die I Die II

Die. The original piece of metal or other material on which the stamp's design is first engraved and from which reproductions are made to form the printing unit. When a die is altered the original is called Die I and later versions Die II, III, etc., to differentiate them. Stamps printed from such dies also bear these designations.
Illustration : Georgian D3 'Key Type' Dies I and II.

Discount Postage. Several countries have experimented with the issue of stamps at a reduced price, chiefly for publicity purposes.

Stamps of Turkey overprinted with an Arabic 'B' (Behié = discount) were sold to business firms at a reduction of 20 per cent below face value, for use on foreign correspondence, the object being to induce people to use the Turkish Post Office in preference to those established in the Levant by other European powers.
Illustration : D4

Persian stamps overprinted 'Relais', etc., were used for letters dropped in boxes at the horse-posting stages between Resht and Teheran. They were supplied to the heads of the posting stages at 10 per cent below face and the overprint was necessary to prevent their resale to merchants in the towns at a discount. *Illustration: D5.*

Doctor Blade. The flexible steel blade which removes surplus ink from the printing cylinder on high speed modern presses. Faulty operation can cause non-constant flaws on the printed stamps.

Double Image. A shadow impression which can occur in offset lithography due to the rubber blanket stretching at the commencement of a printing run.

Double Print. In 1876 Sweden issued a 20 öre very pale orange stamp. The colour faded so badly that the sheets were withdrawn and printed a second time in vermilion, over the first impression. On sheets which were inaccurately registered both impressions are visible. This is described as a Double Print and should not be confused with 'Double Impression' which describes an unintentional doubling during printing. *Illustrations: D6, Sweden 20 öre very pale orange: D7, Double print, pale orange and vermilion.*

Duty Plate. A technical term applied to the plate used to print the value or the name and value on stamps printed at two operations. A separate Duty Plate is needed for every value, but the plate which prints the general design is constant throughout and is called the 'Key Plate' or 'Head Plate'.

Illustration: D8, Key Plate section obliterated to show Duty Plate.

Entire. An envelope, postcard or wrapper, with stamps affixed or printed on it to prepay postage. Not applicable to pre-adhesive covers.

Erased. Stamps have been issued by various countries with parts of the design or overprint removed, generally by erasing the unwanted part on the printing plate, and sometimes on the stamp itself.

Error Erased. On sheets of Italian stamps surcharged for use in the Levant in 1908, one stamp was inadvertently surcharged '20 PIASTRE' instead of '2 PIASTRE' and the unwanted '0' was simply scraped out on the stamp itself. *Illustration: E1.*

Partly Erased. In the issue of Bavarian stamps overprinted in 1920 for use throughout the whole of Germany, the word 'BAYERN' was partly erased from the plate of the 20m. before printing the stamps to be overprinted. This was done to make the overprint legible.
Illustrations: E3, Original stamp; E4, Partly erased and overprinted.

E5

E6

E7

E8

E9

E10

E11

E12

E13

E14

E15

E16

E17

E18

E19

E20

E21

E24

E22

E23

E25

E26

E27

E28

E29

E30

Value Erased. In the Argentine state of Corrientes from 1860 to 1880, various issues of stamps comprising three values, were made in different colours.These stamps bore no impressed value, the value tablet being left blank owing to the erasure of the original value from the plate as previously used.
Illustration : E2, Corrientes 1867 (2c.) *black on lemon-yellow.*

Error. A stamp which, inadvertently, has something abnormal about its production, but which has been issued by a postal authority. Not to be confused with Flaws or Varieties which occur during printing due to faulty workmanship.

Design Error. Errors may arise on stamps when the artist prepares his artwork. Two well-known examples are shown.
Illustrations: E9, Newfoundland 1928 1c. Cape Bauld and Cape Norman transposed; E10, Corrected; E11, Jamaica 1921 2½d. *Union Jack at left inverted; E12, Corrected.*

Error of Colour. Sheets of stamps are sometimes printed in the wrong colour by mistake, and in some cases, sheets which Postal Authorities have been experimenting with, are issued to the public in error. It may also happen that a cliché of a different value is accidentally built into a plate during manufacture and the stamp printed from this is in the wrong colour for that value.
Illustrations: E5, E7, Error; E6, E8, Normal.

'Official' Error. On one or two sheets of the 1937 50 l. Greek Red Cross stamp the overprint was accidentally inverted, and stamps from these sheets were sold at post offices before being discovered. To prevent speculation the Postal Authorities deliberately printed a further supply with the overprint inverted and placed them on sale at the chief post offices.
Illustrations: E13–14, Error and normal.

Paper Error. Stamps printed on paper of the wrong colour (intended for another value); or printed on paper specially watermarked for another value or issue.
Illustrations: E15, Hungary 1913 60 f. olive-green on white; E16, 60 f. olive-green on rose: E17–18 New South Wales 1862 2d., Error Watermark '5': Normal Watermark '2'.

Perforation Error. Caused by sheets of stamps passing through a perforating machine of a different gauge than that specified for the issue, or by passing through the machine more than once.
Illustrations: E19–20.

Printing Error. Usually due to mistakes made in feeding the paper into the printing machine, e.g. inverted, reversed, twice, etc.; or to mistakes made when making the printing or overprinting plate.
Illustrations: E21, Double surcharge, E22, Inverted surcharge; E23, Double overprint, once inverted; E24 Cliché for 8a, frame inserted in 6a. plate; E25, Inverted overprint; *E26, Double and misplaced overprint; E27, Colours* (*including value*) *omitted; E28, 'Ealf-Pence'* (*'E' for 'H' in 'Half'*)*; E29, Double sheet number; E30, Double impression.*

Error of perforation

Illustrations: E31, Cliche for Mozambique stamp inserted in plate of Cape Verde; E32, Inverted centre; E33, Corner figures and inscriptions doubly impressed, once inverted; E34, Value omitted; E35, Wrong date in surcharge (should be '1930').

Watermark Error. Errors may be found in actual watermarks, for example, a third rose instead of a thistle in the 'Emblems' watermark of Great Britain 1885, but there are other errors due to mistakes in feeding the paper into the printing machine which cause the watermark to appear incorrectly in relation to the design of the stamp. A watermark should appear normal when seen through the face of the stamp, therefore reversed when looked at from the back. In cases where the design of a watermark consists of a symmetrical device only, no obvious difference would be detected.

Normal

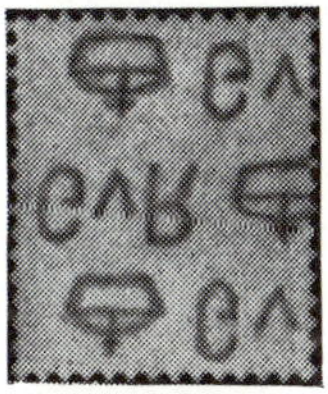

Inverted

Reversed

Reversed and inverted

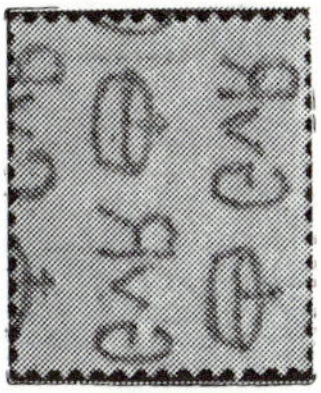

Sideways

Sideways inverted

E31

E32

E33

E34

E35

E36

E37

E38

E39

E40

E41

E42

E43

E44

E45

E46

E47

E48

E49

E50

E51

Essay. A design which has been submitted for a stamp, but not adopted, or has been adopted after alterations have been made.
Illustrations: E36, Andorra; E37, Great Britain (Treasury Competition Essay); E38, Denmark.

Three of David Gentleman's essays for the 1970 Philympia stamps of Great Britain. A 'dreadful warning' version, included to show the bad effect of a coloured background on this particular set of designs, but not submitted as a genuine design for consideration.

Europa. Issues made by certain European countries since 1956 (often with a common motif) to further the project of a United Europe and to commemorate the annual European Postal and Telecommunications Conference.

The 1969 Great Britain 'Europa' stamp also marked the Tenth Annual CEPT Conference.

Expedition Stamps. ***Scientific Expeditions.*** Stamps issued for the use of members of official expeditions of exploration, e.g. the Shackleton Antarctic Expedition of 1908 to King Edward VII Land and the Scott Antarctic Expedition of 1911 to Victoria Land. These issues were authorised by the New Zealand Post Office and franked correspondence to New Zealand.
Illustrations: E39–40.

Military Expeditions. Stamps issued to military forces on foreign service, e.g. Indian troops in China during the Boxer Rising, and during the First World War. Liberia issued stamps overprinted 'L.F.F.' (Liberian Field Force) about 1915 for use by a punitive expedition sent against natives.
Illustrations: E41–3.

Expatriated Post. When Germany occupied Belgium during the 1914–18 War, the Belgian government was moved into France and continued to function in a limited fashion from the port of Le Havre. The Belgian postal service also continued and, as a special concession, the use of Belgian stamps was allowed in Le Havre and they were accepted for the prepayment of postage. The postmark is their only distinguishing feature.
Illustration: E44.

During the 1939–45 War, as various countries were overrun by the Axis powers, their governments were transferred to Britain. Poland, Norway and Yugoslavia, under their rights as members of the Universal Postal Convention, issued stamps for use on their naval vessels. The expatriate Czech government was granted the use of a postmark commemorating the twenty-third anniversary of the foundation of the Czechoslovak Republic, for use on letters from Czech forces stationed in Britain.
Illustrations: E45–7, Poland; E48–9, Norway; E50, Yugoslavia, E51, Czech postmark.

Express Stamps. Stamps specially issued to affix to letters, etc., which are to be delivered by express messenger on payment of an additional fee. Special Delivery stamps are similar.
Illustrations: E52, China 1909 *stamp in four parts* (*one of the world's largest*), *demonetised in 1916 and became merely receipts without franking value; E53, Mauritius* (*foreign mail*)*; E54, Mauritius* (*inland mail*)*; E55, Canada; E56, Spain* (*Red Cross*)*; E57, Philippine Islands* (*Official*).

Express Air Mail. Express stamps specially provided for mail carried by air services.
Illustration: E60, Italy.

E52

E53

E54

E55

E56

E57

E58

E59

E60

E61

E62

F1

F2

F3

F4

F5

F6

F7

F8

F9

F10

Express Newspaper and Printed Matter Post. Stamps for the express delivery of newspapers or commercial printed matter.
Illustration: E61, Czechoslovakia.

Express Parcel Post. Stamps of the same character as letter express stamps, but for use on parcels.
Illustration: E62, Vatican City.

Personal Delivery. Two special stamps were provided in Czechoslovakia in 1937 to ensure a greater degree of certainty of delivery.
Illustration: E58, 50 h. carmine, represented a special fee payable by an addressee who required all his mail to be delivered to him personally. It was affixed by the Post Office delivering such mail.

E59, 50 h. blue, prepaid a special additional fee which ensured personal delivery to the addressee. It was affixed by the sender.

Fake. Used to describe a genuine stamp which has been 'doctored' (by altering its colour, perforation, postmark, etc.) in order to defraud; this term is *not* synonymous with 'Forgery'.

Cleaned. Stamps which have had ink, fiscal or other cancellation removed by chemical or other agency.
Illustrations: F1, Natal, fiscal cancellation removed and forged postmark added; F2, Cape of Good Hope, cancellation removed.

Colour. Faking of colours is usually effected chemically; a rare shade may be produced from a common one, or colours can be changed entirely.
Illustrations: F4, United States, normal colour; F5, similar stamp with colour changed by chemical action (a 'colour changeling').

Perforation. Amongst perforation fakes to be found are imperforate stamps perforated, perforations removed and wide imperforate margins added, gauge of perforation altered, etc.

Illustrations: F3, New South Wales, perforated stamp made imperf; F6, China, faked to represent 'imperf between pair'; F7, Great Britain 1s. green, normal wing-margined stamp and similar stamp with margin removed and edge perforated.

Repaired. The repairs effected extend to adding faked margins and to painting-in missing portions of torn or badly damaged specimens. Many such repaired stamps can only be detected by the most minute examination by experts.
Illustrations: F8, Finland, roulette repaired; F9, Great Britain, borders painted in; F10, Newfoundland, top perforation added.

Flaw—diaeresis over 'A' on South Africa's 12½ c. Antarctic Treaty stamp

Fiscal Stamps. Revenue stamps used for the collection of taxes or fees for non-postal purposes, as opposed to postage or telegraph stamps which are employed for payment of the transmission of an item through the postal service.
Illustrations: F11, Canada; F12, South Africa; F13, Guernsey; F14, New South Wales.

Flaw. A fortuitous blemish upon the design of a stamp or its perforation, which has arisen in the course of manufacture. Such flaws may be caused by ink crusts or foreign matter on the printing plate, or by a fold in the paper and are frequently transient. When a flaw is constant, that is, repeats throughout an issue of stamps or part of an issue, it may be termed a variety (*F15*).
Illustrations: F15, Aden, flaw on wall on top left stamp (see below); F16, New South Wales, white flaw caused by paper crease; F17, Rumania, 'ring flaw' caused by foreign matter on plate; F18, Ukraine, blank corner caused by intervening paper; F19, France, perforation flaw caused by paper fold.

Flaw *Normal*

Foreign Mail Stamps. Various countries have issued two series of postage stamps, one intended for the prepayment of postage on mail to be sent out of the country, and the other for delivery of mail within the national boundary (Inland Mail Stamps).
Illustrations: F20, Haiti; F21, Turkey; F22, Guatemala.

Forgery. An imitation of a stamp intended to deceive. Where a genuine stamp bears a forged postmark or overprint, etc., it should be described as 'genuine, with forged cancellation (etc.)'.
Illustrations: F23, Western Australia forgery; F24, Chile, genuine stamp with forged 'OFFICIAL' overprint.

F11

F12

F13

F14

F15

F16

F17

F18

F19

F20

F21

F22

F23

F24

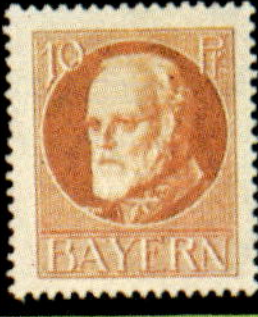

F25

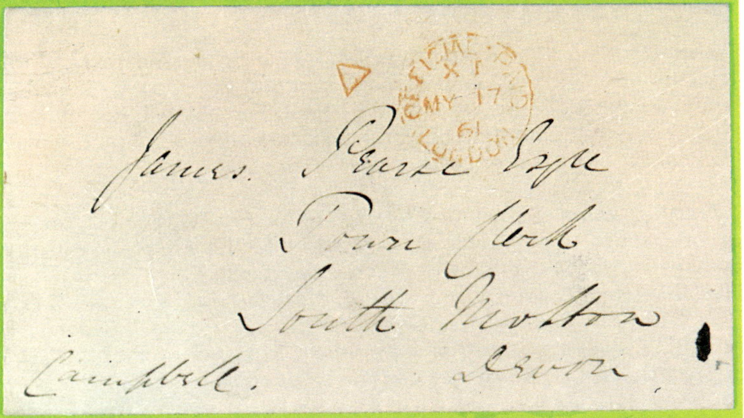

F26

F27

F28

F29

F30

F31

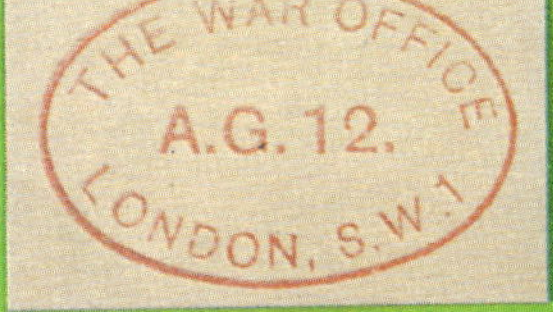

F32

Postal Forgery. Forged stamps prepared and used to defraud the postal authorities.

Propaganda Forgery. Stamps forged in Britain during the two World Wars and smuggled into enemy territory to be used by Allied agents. Designs distorted for propaganda purposes (by both sides) were not intended for postal use and would be better described as propaganda labels.
Illustration: F25, Bavaria, World War One forgery.

Frank. Meaning 'Free (of postage)'. In Great Britain Members of Parliament and other privileged persons could at one time, by signature, 'frank' a letter to be delivered free by post. Forces Mail, posted in the field of action during time of war, also passes free through the mails.
Illustration: F26, Franked cover, signed 'Campbell'.

Frank Stamps. Sometimes referred to as 'Private Stamps', they are usually issued to charitable or national institutions and show that no postage is payable on items to which they are affixed.
Illustrations: F27, Switzerland, Charity Hospital; F28, Portugal, Civilian Rifle Club; F29, Portugal, Red Cross Society; F30, Portugal, Geographical Society; F31, Spain, issued by government to author of book on history of Spanish stamps, which was considered of public utility.

Handstamped Frank. Used by various British and other government departments.
Illustration: F32.

Postal Frank. Before the island of Madagascar was annexed by the French in 1896, the British Vice-Consulate in Antananarivo sold franks to inland residents to facilitate business. These Postal Franks were only attached to letters by the gummed corner and obviated the necessity of remitting money in payment of postage. On receipt of letters by the Consulate post, the franks were removed and the letters forwarded to the postmaster at Port Louis, where they were franked with the appropriate Mauritius or Reunion stamps, and the amount debited to the Vice-Consulate at Antananarivo.
Illustrations: F33–34.

Fugitive Colours. Inks with fugitive colours are specially prepared to print some stamps so that they will change, fade or wash out if any attempt is made to tamper with the stamp (remove the postmark, etc.).
Illustrations: F35–37.

Graphite Lines. Vertical graphite lines printed in black (beneath the gum) of certain British stamps in 1957. These were used in connexion with automatic sorting machinery, first introduced experimentally at Southampton.

Graphite lines (from back of stamps), one line only on 2d., as shown.

Greetings Stamps. Special stamps printed, or ordinary stamps overprinted, conveying Christmas or New Year Greetings.
Illustrations: G1, Manchukuo (New Year); G2, Paraguay (Christmas); G3, United States.

Grille. A security device in the form of small square dots embossed on certain stamps of the United States, Peru, etc. They can be arranged in a square or diamond, or even cover the whole area of the stamps, breaking the paper fibres. This allows the ink of the postmark to soak in deeply and makes it impossible to clean a stamp for re-use.
Illustrations: G4, United States; G5, Peru.

Guide Lines and Dots. Fine lines or dots marked upon the printing plate as a guide for the engraver or workman when transferring impressions. Normally these are removed after laying down the plate, but they are sometimes still visible on unprinted portions of the design or in the stamp's margin.
Illustration: G6, Great Britain 2s. 6d. with Guide Dot centrally placed above top frame line.

Gum. The adhesive substance usually found on the back of postage stamps when sold to the public. In this state they are described as with 'full O.G.' (original gum). A 'regummed' stamp has had fresh gum added to give the impression that it is 'O.G.'. The colour or type of adhesive used is sometimes of value to differentiate between two issues or printings.
Illustrations: G7, Crackled Gum; G8, Yellow Gum; G9, White Gum; G10, Rose Gum.

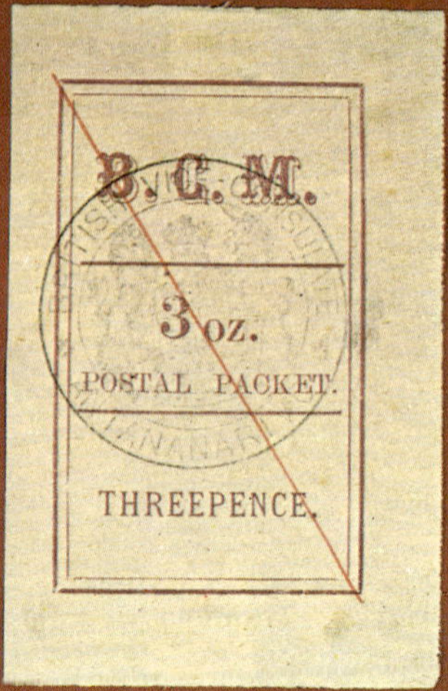

F33

F34

F35

F36

F37

G1

G2

G3

G4

G5

G6

G7

G8

G9

G10

G11

G12

H1

H2

H3

I1

I2

H4

I3

I4

I5

Gutter. Space left between stamps to allow them to be separated or perforated.
Illustrations: G11, Narrow Gutter, 2½mm; G12, Wide Gutter, 3½mm.

Gutter Margin. The margin dividing a sheet of stamps into separate panes.

Hair Lines. The name given to the diagonal white lines which cross the outer corners of certain early British surface-printed stamps. In these cases they distinguish the impressions from particular plates of these issues. Also used to describe fine cracks or scratches on a printing plate or cylinder which print in colour on stamps or sheet margins (e.g. Canada 1912 1 c. and 2 c.). It is incorrect to use this term to describe 'Guide Lines'.
Illustration: H1, Great Britain 4d. with Hair Lines in each corner.

Handstamp. A postmark or overprint applied by hand—'handstamped'.
Illustration: H3, Haiti.

Handstruck. An impression manually produced from a single die attached to a handle. Examples of 'handstruck adhesives' are the Postmaster's stamps of Bermuda and the early circular stamps of Afghanistan.

The term 'Handstruck stamps' is also used to describe markings applied to letters prior to the use of adhesive postage stamps, to indicate that postage had been paid.
Illustration: H2, Afghanistan.

Health Stamps. Stamps bearing an additional charity premium, proceeds from which are devoted to the promotion of health.
Illustration: H4, New Zealand 1970 Health Stamp.

Imitation Stamps. Governments who wish to repeat certain stamps, usually for sale or distribution to collectors, but find that the original printing plates are no longer available, can have imitations made of these previous issues which are then termed 'Official Imitations' as distinct from 'Reprints'. Variations of design, size and paper are usually found in these Imitations.
Illustrations: I1–2, Original stamps of Wenden and Persia; I3–4, Official Imitations (note differences in size and engraving).

Facsimile. An imitation. Usually applied to imitation stamps which are sold as such. The word or its foreign equivalent may be found either overprinted or incorporated in the design.
Illustration: I5, United States newspaper stamp facsimile (overprinted).

The world's first stamp—the Penny Black—was imperforate. This rare marginal block came from the 'Maximus' Collection

Imperforate. Stamps printed in sheets without perforation or other means of separation, except by the use of knife or scissors. The early stamp issues of numerous countries in the mid-nineteenth century were imperforate. 'Imperf' is permissible, not 'imperforated'. Wide margins are desirable, to allay suspicion of a trimmed (perforated) stamp.
Illustration: I6, Hanover imperforate.

Imperf. Between. Normally perforated, but with a line of perforations inadvertently omitted between adjoining stamps or rows of stamps, due to faulty manufacture. Can apply to horizontal or vertical rows.
Illustrations: I7, Surinam, and I8, Mexico imperf between.

I6

I9

I7

I8

I10

I11

I12

I13

I14

J1

J2

J3

K1

L1

L2

L3 L4 L5

Imprimatur. The first sheets of early British stamps printed from an approved and finished printing plate, or stamps from such a sheet, produced on watermarked paper in the appropriate colour and recorded prior to the general sale of the stamps.
Illustration: I9, Imprimatur of GB One Penny of 1880.

Imprint. The name of the printer or issuing authority inscribed or printed on the sheet margins, or on the stamps themselves. In some cases the names of the designer and/or engraver are included in the stamp designs.
Illustration: I10, Canada 'Coronation' stamps with marginal imprint of the Canadian Bank Note Company; I11, Malagasy Republic (French) imprint on stamp; I12, Bradbury Wilkinson imprint on South West African stamp margin.

Inland Mail Stamps. Some countries, such as Madagascar (now Malagasy Republic), issued special stamps for mail due to be delivered within the national boundaries, i.e. 'inland mail'.
Illustrations: I13, Madagascar 'British Inland Mail' stamp issued by British Vice-Consul of Antananarivo in 1895; I14, Liberian 'Inland Postage' stamp of 1897.

Jubilee Issue. The title popularly (but erroneously) applied to the GB Queen Victoria definitives of 1887, the year of the Queen's Jubilee. The term is frequently used to describe commemorative stamps of other countries.
Illustration: J1, GB 2½d. 'Jubilee' stamp.

Jubilee Line. A continuous or broken coloured line (printer's rule) bordering the stamps in the margin of a sheet or pane, used extensively on GB issues since its introduction in 1887, Queen Victoria's Jubilee year, and on many British Commonwealth issues. The brass rules relieved pressure on the printing plates. Now known as 'marginal rule'.
Illustrations: J2, British Honduras, continuous rule; J3, British Solomon Islands, broken or 'co-extensive' rule.

Key Plate. The plate which prints the general design on stamps, specifically certain British Commonwealth issues, requiring two separate printings, used in conjunction with a separate and variable 'Duty Plate' (which see). Also known as 'Head Plate' as it usually bears the head of the reigning sovereign.
Illustration: K1, Stamp with Duty Plate section obliterated to show Key Plate.

Labelled Stamps. Several countries have issued stamps with labels attached, denoting some special service. Other countries have sought to increase their revenues by the sale of advertising space on stamp margins.

Advertising Labels. Some British stamp booklets have stamp-size advertisements incorporated in the panes of stamps. Italy issued stamps with advertisements attached, without dividing perforation, and other Continental countries have experimented with attached advertising labels.
Illustrations: L1, Belgium 'Farrand'; L2, Belgium 'Persil'; L3, Ireland Telephones; L4, Italy 'Reinach'; L5, G.B. Savings.

Charity Labels. Stamps exist which have the lower margin extended in the form of a label or tab, bearing details of an extra charge for charitable purposes, e.g. the relief of Belgian and Hungarian flood victims, help for children and the aged in Germany.
Illustrations: L6, Belgium, L7 Hungary; L8, Germany.

Dominical Labels. Small, detachable labels attached at the foot of Belgian stamps from 1893 to 1914 which bear the instruction in French and Flemish—'Do not deliver on Sunday'.
Illustration: L9 'Ne pas livrer le dimanche' etc.

Fiscal Labels. The lower label, or coupon, on the stamps of Sonora issued in 1913, was supposed to be removed before the stamps were sold for postal purposes, but have been found postally used with the label attached.
Illustration: L10, Mexico (Sonora).

Labels. Various types of label are to be found on letters and postal packets. Some are official, denoting a special service, others are of a private and unofficial nature.

Air Mail. Labels supplied by the post offices of various countries for affixing to airmail correspondence. In most countries of the world, these labels are deemed sufficient distinction for this class of mail, and special stamps need not specifically be used. Also known by the French term 'Etiquette'.

Illustrations: L11, South African; L12, Dutch; L13, French; L14, Mexican; L15, Air France.

Air Mail (Postally Used). In the Portuguese Colony of Mozambique, airmail labels issued in 1932 were provided with a space for the insertion of the air fee. The amount, completed by postal officials, varied according to the weight of the letter, distance carried and rate of exchange. In 1937, the air fee was combined with the postal charge, and no franking stamps were required, the label being cancelled in the normal manner. *(ill. p. 56).*

L6

L7

L8

L9

L10

L11

L12

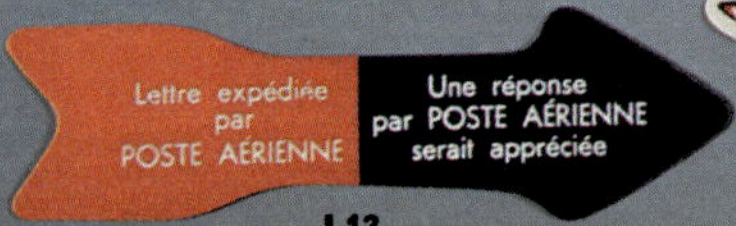

L13

L14

L15

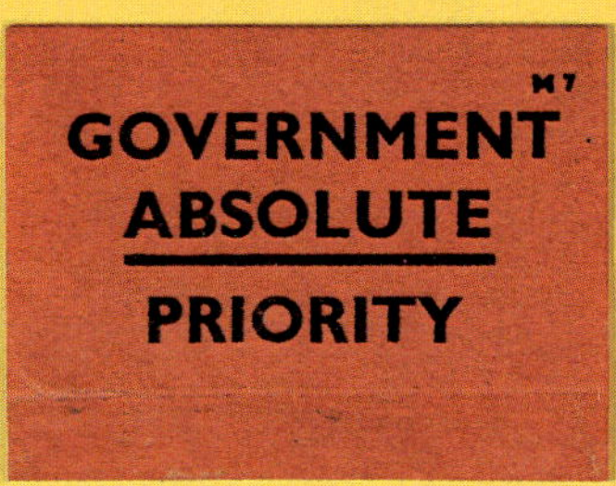

L16

L17

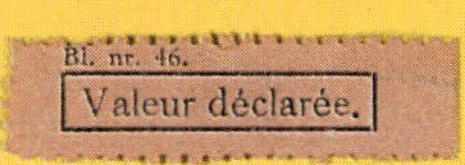

L18

L19

L20

L21

L22

L23

L24

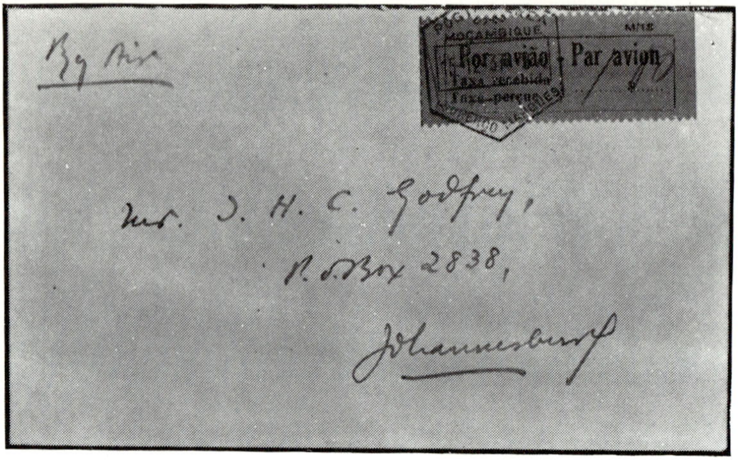

Express. Labels issued by Post Offices for use on letters and telegrams.
Illustrations: L16, L17.

Fiscal. Labels affixed to postal packets by the Customs authorities, denoting that such mail has been examined and passed by them.
Illustration: L18.

Registration. Labels usually printed in blue or red, incorporating the letter 'R' or its foreign equivalent, affixed by postal officials to packets which have been 'registered' for safe transit. These labels bear the name of the issuing office and a serial number which is that of the particular letter or packet.
Illustrations: L19, South Georgia; L20, Prague.

Registration (Provisional). Labels for registration issued in temporary post offices, or for use during a shortage of the normal labels.
Illustrations: L21, British Association (Dundee); L22, Field Post Office.

Registration (Postally Used). Persian postmasters have to account for registration labels at the rate of 1 chahi each, and their use as 1 ch. stamps has often been sanctioned during a shortage of the normal stamps. They were used singly or in multiples, e.g. 1 ch. with a 5 ch. stamp, or 6 × 1 ch. making up the inland rate of 6 ch.
Illustration: L23, Perse (Persia).

Registration labels of German New Guinea were overprinted and surcharged for use as postage stamps, when British forces occupied that Colony in 1914.
Illustration: L24, Rabaul.

Distinctive cachet used by Wells Fargo, most famous of the US 'Carriers'

Sealing. Gummed-paper labels, used by postal authorities to seal open letters, or those which have been opened for censorship, security, customs or re-addressing purposes, or affixed to denote some special service, but not the prepayment of, or payment for postage.
Illustration: L25, A Transvaal letter opened and sealed by the authorities at Durban (top) and Cape Town (side) during the Boer War.

Testing Labels for Automatic Vending Machines. Stamp-size gummed labels issued in coils or rolls by the British Post Office for the use of mechanics testing automatic stamp-vending machines. Not available to the public, but some of the original, green 'poached egg'' labels were inadvertently left in a machine, purchased and used for postage. On this occasion the Post Office authorised their use, but the design was changed to one with a printed explanation of their purpose.
Illustrations: L26, 'Poached egg' labels and, L27, the later 'testing' labels.

Unofficial and Private. Many types of labels are to be found affixed to postal packets, letters and cards, etc., which are purely of a private character and are not valid for postal use. They are usually issued by societies, charitable organisations, exhibitions and hotels etc., for commemorative, philanthropical or propaganda purposes.
Illustrations: L28, Jamaica War Fund; L29, Mount Everest Expedition; IMABA Stamp Exhibition; L31, Hospital Charity; L32, Philatelic Congress; L33, Philatelic War Fund.

Local Stamps. Postage stamps whose validity and use are limited in area to a prescribed district, town or country, or on certain postal routes where there is no official service, issued by civic municipalities, private firms and landowners, etc., sometimes in conjunction with official postal administrations.
Illustrations: L34, Göteborg; L35, Stockholm; L36, Glasgow 'Circular Delivery'.

Carriers' Stamps. Supplementary stamps, such as those issued in the United States, 1849–58, and elsewhere, representing the letter-carriers' charge for conveying mail to or from local post offices. In the U.S. in the early days of the official postal services, letters were transported between post offices only, and private arrangements had to be made for the collection and/or delivery of letters at one's nearest office.
Illustration: L37, U.S. 'P.O. Despatch'.

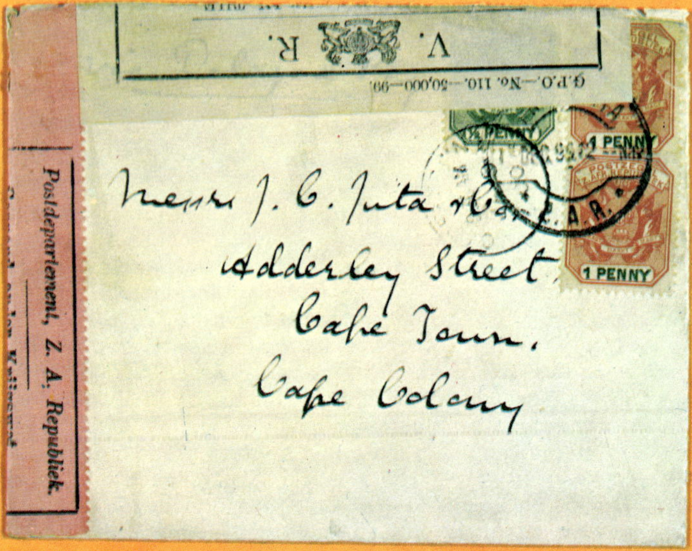

L25

L26

L27

L28

L29

L30

L31

L32

L33

L34

L35

L36

L37

L38

L39

L40

L41

L42

L43

L44

College Stamps. Private stamps issued by some of the Oxford and Cambridge Colleges between 1871 and 1886 for their inter-college messenger services, eventually stopped after intervention by the Post Office.
Illustrations: L38, St John's, Oxford; L39, Selwyn, Cambridge; L40, St John's 'Messenger'; L41, Queen's, Cambridge.

Postmasters' Stamps. Postage stamps issued by the postmasters of certain towns and cities in the U.S. and elsewhere, to facilitate the prepayment of postage, prior to the introduction of issues authorised by the Government. Rare examples are the Perot and Thies (Bermuda) issues of 1848–61.
Illustration: L42, Memphis, Tennessee (Confederate States).

New York Postmaster's Stamp, 1845

Bermuda 'Perot'

Alexandria Postmaster's Stamp, 1846

Shipping Companies' Stamps. As the name indicates, stamps issued by shipping firms to prepay postage on letters carried by their mail-ships or packet-boats between certain ports. The most famous examples are the 5 c. stamps issued by David Bryce, owner of the S.S. *Lady McLeod*, for the prepayment of the carriage of letters between Port of Spain and San Fernando in April 1847, generally accepted as Trinidad's first stamps.
Illustration: L43, Royal Mail Steam Packet Company.

Trinidad 'Lady McLeod' on piece

Zemstvo Issues. The name given to the local posts and stamps of towns and districts in Russia beyond the scope of the Imperial postal services, from 1870 to about 1890. A 'zemstvo' was the administrative centre of a district and a province.
Illustration: L44.

Margin. The paper bordering the printed stamps in a sheet, also the borders of the stamps themselves. See also 'Imprint' and 'Marginal Inscriptions'.
Illustrations: M1, Tokelau Islands, perforated through top margin; M2, Rwanda, inscribed margin.

Gutter Margin. The margin or space between panes of stamps in a sheet. They may be found with or without a printed pattern. 'Gutter' also applies to the narrow margins between stamps in a pane or sheet which are normally perforated.
Illustration: M3, Leeward Islands.

Wing Margin. An extra wing or 'flap' of the margin forming part of the stamp, i.e. perforated on its outside edge, caused when the vertical gutters of sheets of stamps were perforated centrally instead of close to the divided stamps.
Illustration: M4, G.B. 1s. of 1872—a reconstructed pair.

MI

M2

M3

M4

M5

M6

M8

M9

M7

M10 M11 M12

Marginal Guide Marks. Lines, dots, arrows and other marks in the margins of sheets of stamps serving as a guide for the printer in perforating and trimming the printed sheets.
Illustrations: M5, Malta, intersecting lines.

Electric Eye Marks. Marginal marks on sheets of stamps to ensure accurate perforation, alignment being controlled by a photo-electric device—the 'Electric Eye'—which 'reads' the marks.
Illustration: M6, United States.

Part of the marginal inscription on the Great Britain Penny Black

Marginal Inscriptions. 'Printed matter' appearing on the margins of sheets of stamps. The inscriptions range from the name of the issuing authority, the printer's name or trading style (known as the 'imprint'), cylinder, plate or control numbers, to instructions on the use of the stamps, the total face value of the sheet, and of its separate columns or rows.
Illustrations: M7, British East Africa; M8, France; M9, Germany.

Metal Currency Stamps. Some postage stamps could only be purchased by silver; others required payment at the current 'gold' exchange rate. In Peru (1880), paper money depreciated so much that the current stamps were overprinted with a device inscribed 'Plata' (silver, in Spanish) indicating that payment had to be made in silver. On Greek stamps, the inscribed or overprinted letters 'AM' stand for 'Axia Metallike' or 'Metal (i.e. gold) Value', meaning that the stamps, intended for foreign parcels, had to be paid for at the 'gold' exchange rate.
Illustrations: M10, Peru, 'Plata'; M11, Greece, 'AM' inscribed, and, M12 overprinted.

*Swiss Mobile Post Office stamps—
winter and summer landscapes*

Metered Mail. Mail which is automatically franked by a machine. The franked impression, which is a combined 'postage stamp and postmark', marks the amount of postage paid and the date of posting, while the automatic machine 'meters' or records the number of letters and the total postage. Metered mail is used extensively by large public organisations and commercial houses who lease their own machines, and whose meter marks invariably include advertisements or slogans.
Illustration: M13

Military Service Stamps. Also known as 'Military Franks', these are specially overprinted stamps issued by various countries to members of the fighting services, indicating that postage is free or at a reduced rate on mail sent home. No such stamps are used in the British services, although special stamps were issued by the Egyptian Government when the Army was in Egypt. *See below.*
Illustrations: M14, France—'Franchise Militaire'; M15, Japan—military frank; M16, Denmark, 'Soldater Frimærke'.

Egyptian Army Post. Between 1932 and 1936, members of the British Forces in Egypt and their families were permitted to send letters to the UK at reduced rates. Special seals sold at NAAFI Institutes and canteens were used in lieu of Egyptian stamps, and these were affixed on the back of the envelopes, which were handstamped on the front 'Egypt Postage Prepaid' in a double circle surmounted by a crown. These labels were replaced by special stamps from 1 March 1936.
Illustration: M17, 'Army Post' stamp.

Millésime. Numerals recording the year of printing certain stamps of France and Colonies—'1', '2', etc. (the last digit of the year of issue), usually printed in the gutter margins between panes.
Illustrations: M18, France 1900–24: M19, French Morocco 1915.

Mobile Post Office Stamp. In various countries, motor coaches or vans are equipped as 'travelling post offices', providing postal services at outdoor events such as agricultural and sports meetings. In Switzer-

M13

M14

M15

M16

M17

M18

M19

M20

M21

M22

M23

M24

M25

M26

M27

N1

N2

N3

N4

N5

N6

N7

land, cross-country services are operated by the well-known yellow motor coaches for which special stamps are issued. Tram-cars in Amsterdam and other Continental cities are fitted with mail collection boxes. In most cases, the postmark is the only means of identifying such mail.
Illustration : M20, Switzerland.

Moiré. A pattern of close-set wavy lines simulating watered silk, printed on postage stamps as a form of security. Examples may be seen on the backs of Mexican stamps issued in 1872, and overprinted on British Honduras issues during World War I.
Illustration : M21.

Mourning Stamps. Stamps issued on occasions of national bereavement, either special issues printed in black or existing stamps having an added black border.
Illustrations: M22, Lithuania (*Dr Basanavicius*)*; M23, Belgium* (*Queen Astrid*)*; M24, Russia* (*Lenin*).

A stamp from Ceylon inscribed in three languages

Multi-lingual Stamps. Stamps inscribed in more than one language, due to a country's mixed population which may have originated by colonisation or by having been controlled by various foreign governments for certain periods in history. The stamps of Ceylon, for example, were inscribed in English, Singhalese and Tamil.
Illustrations: M25, Persia (*French and Persian—alphabet mainly Perso-Arabic*)*; M26, Egypt* (*French and Arabic*)*; M27, North Borneo* (*English, Malay and Chinese*).

Neurope. A coined word for certain stamps of 'New Europe' issued during and after World War I.
Illustrations: N1, Czechoslovakia; N2, Latvia.

Newspaper Stamps. Stamps issued specifically for the prepayment of postage on newspapers.
Illustrations: N3, Austria (Military Post); N4, United States; N5, New Zealand; N6, Hungary.

Journal Tax Stamps. Stamps representing non-postal newspaper taxes. French stamps issued in 1868, however, incorporated a combined fiscal and postal charge.
Illustration: N7, France 1868.

One of the early issues of Trinidad, where no face value was expressd on the stamps

No Value Expressed. Stamps, such as the early British Colonial issues, printed without any face-value being indicated, the colours alone serving to differentiate between the values in use. See also 'Frank Stamps'.
Illustrations: N8, Barbados; N9, Czechoslovakia (Czech Army in Siberia); N10, Spain, official (value expressed in words—'half ounce').

Numbered Stamps. Certain stamps of Estonia and Uruguay were numbered in rotation, the numbers forming part of the design. Spanish stamps of 1875 (and more recent issues) were numbered on the back.
Illustrations: N11, Uruguay; N12, Spain.

Numerals of Value. The early stamps of Greece had the numerals of value printed on the backs to facilitate easy handling by postal staff.
Illustration: N13.

Obligatory Tax Stamps. Special stamps issued for the collection of funds for national or philanthropic purposes. Their use is usually compulsory on all letters on certain days or during certain periods, in addition to the ordinary postage stamps.
Illustration: O1, Colombia Red Cross.

N8
N9
N10
N11
N12
N13
O1
O2
O3
O4
O5
O6
O7
O8

O9

O10

O11

O12

O13

O14

O15

O16

O17

O18

O19

O20

O21

Sunday Delivery. In Bulgaria, special stamps were issued for use on letters to be delivered on Sundays and holidays. Their use was obligatory, and the funds raised were used for the maintenance of a sanatorium for postal employees.
Illustration: O2.

Obliterated Stamps. On occasion, the stamp portrait of a deposed or deceased monarch or president of a country is blotted out by various devices.
Illustrations: O3, Salvador (Gen. Ezeta); O4, Persia (Sultan Ahmed Shah); O5, Serbia (Alexander I).

Obsolete. Stamps which have ceased to be available for postal use, though possibly continuing to be valid for postage. Stamps which are no longer valid are declared to be 'invalidated' or 'demonetised'.
Illustration: O6, GB King Edward VIII.

Tanganyika 1916. Nyasa-Rhodesian Force overprint

Occupation Stamps. Stamps overprinted, or specially printed, for use in a territory occupied by enemy forces, or through a national or political *coup d'état.* Some are also known as 'Expeditionary Force' stamps, e.g. 'N.F.' opts. of Nyasa-Rhodesian Force in Tanganyika.
Illustrations: O7, Cameroons; O8, Finnish Occupation of Eastern Karelia.

Official Stamps. Stamps specially issued or overprinted for use by governments or government departments.
Illustrations: O9, Liberia; O10, India O11; Spain; O12, Trinidad; O13, Costa Rica; O14, Dominican Republic; O15, Uruguay.

Departmental Stamps. As above, but inscribed for specific departments.
Illustrations: O16, GB Army; O17, US 'Interior'; O18, US Post Office; O19, New Zealand Life Insurance.

Sealing Stamps. Indicating that a letter has been officially opened (and re-sealed).
Illustration: O20, Chile.

Egyptian 'Interpostals'. Stamps without postal validity, used on inter-post office mails, also as 'sealers'.
Illustration: O21.

Samoa—a wartime overprint which is technically a 'surcharge'

Overprint. An additional inscription or device printed on the face of a stamp. If it effects an alteration in the original face value of the stamp, it is generally defined as a 'surcharge', even though there may also be a commemorative inscription in the overprinted matter.
Illustrations: 022, Portuguese Congo 'REPUBLICA'; 023, Peru manuscript; 024, Chile 'CORREO AEREO'; 025, Grenada 'WAR TAX'; 026, Niger 'APOLLO XIII', etc.; 027, Ireland; 028, Uruguay.

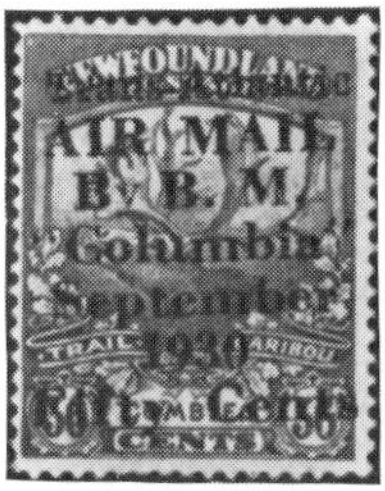

A famous air mail overprint, for the 1930 'Columbia' flight from Newfoundland

Continuous Overprint. A multiple, overall overprint, applied without regard to positioning on the individual stamps in a sheet. The Spanish overprint shown here was repeated 18 times in each vertical row of 10 stamps.
Illustration: 029, Spain 1931 'Republica Española'.

Security Overprint. When some values of the 1934 issue of Macao were overprinted for airmail use, Greek characters were included in order to make forgery more difficult.
Illustration: 030.

Pair of Stamps. Two unseparated stamps, joined horizontally or vertically as originally issued.
Illustrations: P1, South Africa bilingual pair; P2, South West Africa bilingual overprint; P3, G.B. horizontal pair; P4, France vertical pair.

Matched Pair. A term usually applied to G.B. Penny Blacks and Penny Reds printed from the same plate and bearing identical corner letters.
Illustration: P5, Penny Black and Penny Red from Plate VIII showing the 'Q' flaw, corner letters 'EC'.

O22

O23

O24

O25

O26

O27

O28

O29

O30

P1

P2

P3

P4

P5

P6

P7

P8

P9

P10

P11

Paper. In the production of postage stamps, paper plays a very important part—being produced under widely different conditions, it exists in almost endless variety. Broadly speaking, paper for stamps must be suitable for the method of printing employed; of a convenient texture and thickness for handling by the public; and should provide as much protection as possible against forgery of the stamps, or against attempts to clean off postmarks so that the stamps can (illegally) be used again. Apart from the regular types of paper and their variations of quality and thickness, many experimental and makeshift papers are to be found which are of great interest to philatelists.

Bâtonné. A term adapted from the French, denoting paper watermarked with straight parallel lines some distance apart, originally as a handwriting guide. The basic paper may be either 'wove' (plain) or 'laid' (with closely-set parallel lines), known as 'wove bâtonné' or 'laid bâtonné'.
Illustrations: P6, Poonch 1877 (wove); P7, Poonch 1884 (laid).

Blue Safety Paper. The name given to paper used for some of the early British postage and fiscal stamps. The paper had prussiate of potash added to it during manufacture—this prevented the printing ink from penetrating deeply into the paper so that any attempt to remove the postmark removed the design as well. The blueness, quite unintentional, was due to chemical reaction. See 'Blued Paper'.
Illustration: P8, G.B. fiscal.

A pair of Great Britain 1841 1d. red-brown (S.G.8a) which were printed on very blue paper

Blued Paper. Also 'bleuté'. Paper which has a pale blue tinge, caused by ingredients used in the manufacture of the printing ink and/or paper, or by the chemical reaction of one on the other.
Illustration: P9, G.B. Penny Red.

Cardboard. Fine-quality card of varying degrees of thickness is used for proofing impressions of stamp dies and plates, and imprinted 'stamps' are used on postcards. Thick, semi-card paper, also known as 'carton paper', has been used for adhesive stamps.
Illustration: P10, G.B. imprinted 'stamp'.

Cartridge Paper. Certain paper originally used in the manufacture of cartridges, but the name now covers a wide range of papers employed mainly for drawing purposes. Rarely used for stamps.
Illustration : P11, Russia.

Chalk-surfaced Paper. This is paper coated with a chalky solution for security purposes—the postmark cannot be removed without causing damage to the surface of the stamp. Chalky paper has a sheen and may be distinguished by a simple test—touched with silver (a coin, for example), a kind of 'pencil' mark is caused.
Illustration : P12, Dominica.

Coloured Papers. Used for a great variety of stamps to assist in the identification of different stamp values. Such papers may be divided into three classes. (1) Coloured. Produced at the pulp stage of manufacture and coloured throughout (front and back of the stamps); (2) Surface coloured. Paper coloured on the surface (or front) only, after manufacture, usually with 'white back'; (3) Tinted. Paper slightly toned or shaded.
Illustrations : P13 (1), St Vincent ; P14 (1), British Honduras ; P15 (2), French Guinea ; P16 (2), Russia ; P17 (3), Belgium.

These early stamps of Switzerland are printed on 'Silk Thread' paper

Dickinson or Silk Thread Paper. A security paper distinguished by having long silk threads embodied in it. Named after its inventor, John Dickinson, and used in the production of the early G.B. envelopes and the embossed 10d. and 1s. stamps of 1847–54. Similarly used for some of the early issues of the German States and Switzerland.
Illustrations : P18, G.B. embossed envelope ; P19, Switzerland.

Double Paper. Some early stamps of the United States were printed on double paper—a thin, porous paper 'welded' on to a comparatively

P12

P13

P14

P15

P16

P17

P18

P19

P20

P21

P22

P23

P24

P25

P26

P27

P28

P29

P30

thick paper. It was supposed that any attempt to remove a postmark would be likely to destroy the delicate surface paper.
Illustration : P20 (imitation).

Enamelled Paper. Similar in appearance to chalk-surfaced paper, but the coating consists of a solution of zinc white and glue, and is extremely brittle.
Illustration : P21, Portugal.

Glazed Paper. A highly-calendered paper *without* any special coating, sometimes confused with enamel-surfaced paper. Has a considerable gloss.
Illustrations : P22, Portugal ; P23, Russia ; P24, Barwani.

Grand Consommation. During and after World War I, a shortage of the usual wove stamp paper in France led to the emergency use of a pale grey granite paper of inferior quality, also known as 'G.C.' paper from the marginal inscription.
Illustrations : P25/27.

Granite Paper. A colloquial term for paper having coloured cotton, linen, jute or wool fibres embodied within it (in appearance, like the 'veins' in granite), the fibres being introduced in the pulp stage of manufacture. Used for the older stamps of Austria, Switzerland and other countries, also for modern Swiss and China-Formosan stamps, etc. A paper of similar character, known as 'silk paper', was used in the United States for some of their revenue stamps, coloured silk being the fibre used.
Illustrations : P28, Switzerland ; P29, Austria ; P30, U.S. 'inland' revenue—silk fibres.

Granite Paper

Deckle-edged, handmade paper was used for the Penny Black

Hand-made. Paper made by hand in moulds, and thus in separate sheets instead of machine-made continuous reels. The sheets are usually deckle-edged, i.e. rough or untrimmed, due to the uneven deckle or frame of the mould, or the wire-gauge sieve within it. The production of hand-made paper reflects the skill of the craftsman, and there is often variation in thickness, even in the same sheet.
Illustrations: P31, GB Twopence Blue; P32 Travancore; P33, Austria.

Early French handmade paper

India-paper. A thin, soft, absorbent paper, of Chinese or Japanese origin (made from the fibre of bamboo), used in taking the finest proofs from engraved plates; also a thin, tough, opaque paper used for the compact printing of voluminous manuscripts, such as the Bible. Used also for proofing.
Illustration: P34, France 'Mouchon' proof.

Japanese Paper. In early days, the manufacture of paper in Japan was a regular domestic chore. The product was a fine soft paper made from the bark of the mulberry tree, the long fibres accounting for its renowned strength. Found in varying degrees of texture and thickness, wove or laid. Also known as 'native paper'.
Illustrations: P35/36, Japan 'Cherry Blossom' issues of 1872.

P31

P32

P33

P35

P34

P36

P37

P39

P38

P40

P41

P42

P43

P44

P45

P46

P47

P48

P49

P50

P51

P52

P53

P54

P55

P56

P57

P58

Laid Paper. Paper which shows a pattern of watermarked lines set closely together, the lines being caused by the parallel wires forming the base of the mould, or covering the 'dandy-roll' in machine-made paper, and usually crossed by widely-spaced lines. Described as 'vertically laid' or 'horizontally laid' according to the direction of the lines in relation to the design of the stamp.
Illustrations: P37/38, Latvia and Russia, both vertically laid; P39, Latvia, horizontally laid.

Laid Paper

Manilla Paper. A coarse, strong paper of light texture, originally manufactured from Manilla hemp, usually pale brown in colour and with one glazed side. Used in making envelopes and wrappers, also in a heavier weight for postcards.
Illustrations: P40, Egypt; P41, GB. KG V; P42, France.

Native Paper. A general term indicating locally-made paper used for the stamps of some of the Indian States and the Oriental countries. Usually tough and fibrous, varying greatly in texture and thickness.
Illustrations: P43, Tibet; P44, Bhor; P45, Kashmir.

Pelure Paper. A word adapted from the French, meaning a very thin, but also hard and tough paper, usually semi-transparent.
Illustrations: P46, Serbia; P47, Russia.

Porous Paper. Very soft, absorbent paper, usually unglazed.
Illustration: P48, Nicaragua.

Quadrillé Paper. From the French—paper watermarked with criss-cross lines forming a pattern of small squares. A pattern of rectangles is termed 'oblong quadrillé', and some stamps, though described as being on quadrillé paper, merely have a protective coating in such a pattern, called 'surface quadrillé'. The term 'quadrillé' is also used to denote the pattern of small printed squares on album leaves.
Illustrations: P49, Guadalajara (Mexico); P50, Obock ('surface'); P51, Ecuador ('oblong').

Resinised Paper. Thin paper, saturated with resin to render it transparent, also known as 'gold-beater's skin'. Prussian parcel stamps of 1866 had the design printed in a negative impression (i.e. in reverse) on the under-side and were also gummed on the same side. The stamp showed a positive impression on its face and could not be removed without being damaged.
Illustration: P52, U.S. postal-fiscal.

Ribbed Paper. Paper which has a 'corrugated' appearance due to the closely-set parallel ridges on its surface, produced during manufacture by milling or ridging between steel rollers.
Illustration: P53, Austrian Lombardy and Venetia.

Rice Paper. A thin and delicate paper in a variety of textures, made from the sliced pith of the tree *Fatsia papyrifera* found in Taiwan or from other plants or linen trimmings, and sized with rice-water. Salvador's 1 c. stamp of 1889 is the only stamp recorded as printed on rice paper, although local stamps of Taiwan have been printed on the local product.
Illustration: P54, Salvador.

Safety Paper. All paper which has been specially treated in the course of manufacture to prevent forgery or illicit cleaning, removal of postmarks etc. There are several types in addition to those previously described, e.g. Russian stamps bearing intersecting varnish lines on the surface, the varnish preventing the printing ink from penetrating the paper and making it impossible to remove the postmark without also removing part of the design. Austria used a similar method, the paper having diagonal lines of varnish. Some early stamps of Prussia had an invisible burélage which became apparent when attempts were made to clean the stamps.
Illustrations: P55, Prussia; P56, Austria. Both 'burélage revealed'.

P59

P60

P61

P62

P63

P64

P65

P66

P67

P68

P69

P70

P71

P72

P73

P74

P75

P76

Wove Paper. The normal paper, having in its texture the plain mesh of a fine wire-gauge sieve or mould, used extensively in the manufacture of books, notepaper and postage stamps.
Illustrations: P57, Belgium; P58, Bahamas.

Makeshifts. In times of paper shortage, many countries have printed stamps on paper normally used for other puposes.

Banknote Paper. During 1919–20, the postal authorities of Latvia issued various charity stamps printed on the backs of unfinished Bolshevik banknotes. These notes were printed on strips of paper, in three groups of six notes per strip. Before printing the stamps, the strips were cut in half, so that a complete sheet of stamps shows eight whole and two half notes on its back.
Illustrations: P59/61, Latvia 'banknote' stamps.

Cigarette Paper. In 1919, Latvia issued stamps on paper intended for the manufacture of cigarettes.
Illustrations: P62/64, Latvia 'cigarette' stamps.

Coupon Paper. Also in 1919, stamps were printed in Berlin on grey granite paper which had been manufactured for use as ration tickets for the Lithuanian Post Office.
Illustrations: P65/67, Lithuania 'coupon' stamps.

Post Office Forms. During the Mexican Civil War of 1915, the state of Oaxaca issued five postage stamps printed on the backs of official Post Office forms.
Illustrations: Oaxaco (Mexico) P68, Stamp front; P69/70, Stamp backs or forms.

Ruled Paper. Paper ruled with lines as a guide for writing was used for postage stamps in Latvia and Mexico.
Illustrations: P71, 73, Latvia (1919); P72, Mexico (1887).

War Maps. The first stamps issued by Latvia in 1918 were printed in Riga on the backs of German military maps, of which large quantities were available. A complete sheet or map contained 228 stamps.
Illustrations: P74/76.

GB 'Government Parcels' stamp with a difference!—the overprint is inverted

Paraph. A mark or flourish, used in embellishment, or, in the form of initials, as a signature. Found overprinted on Cuban stamps used in Puerto Rico, 1873–6, and on Mexican stamps.
Illustrations: P77, 79, Puerto Rico; P78, Mexico.

Parcel Post Stamps. Postage stamps designated or inscribed for use on parcels. Their issue and use have declined in recent years.
Illustrations: P80, Rumania; P81, Italy; P82, USA; P83, P85, Belgium (Railway parcels service); P84, Uruguay (Agricultural parcels service); P86, 88, Uruguay (inland and foreign parcels); P87, Portugal; P89, 90, San Marino and Italy—the left-hand portion of these types is affixed to the packet-card, the right-hand portion to the receipt.

Pen-cancelled. A stamp officially cancelled or postmarked by pen marks and which has been postally used.
Illustration: P91, Chile.

Penmarked. A stamp defaced by pen marks for other than postal purposes, e.g. fiscal use, documents, bills, receipts, etc.
Illustrations: P92, New Zealand, P93, GB.

Perforated Stamps. Besides the segregation of stamps, various perforation devices are found on them, mostly changing their purpose.
Illustrations: P94, Spain (telegraphs); P95, Salvador (official); P96, Argentina; P97, Tunisia; P98, Uruguay (official).

Perforated Initials. Initial letters perforated or punctured on or through stamps to denote official use as, for example, the 'OS' perforation of certain Australian stamps, and 'SG' or 'AS' (Sudan Government, Army Service) on those of Sudan. Also the initials of private or public concerns, applied to stamps as a precaution against theft.
Illustrations: P99 GB 'G'; P100, Australia 'OS'; P101, Straits Settlements 'B & Co.'; P102, GB 'PAC' (Prudential Assurance Company).

P77
P78
P79
P80
P81
P82
P83
P84
P85
P86
P87
P88
P89
P90
P91
P92
P93

P94

P95

P96

P97

P98

P99

P100

P101

P102

P103

P104

P105

P106

P107

Perforation. A series of holes punched between stamps in the sheet to facilitate separation. In 'rouletting', another form of separation, slits or cuts are made in the paper.

Typical examples of comb and line perforation

Corner intersections: Line (left) and comb (right)

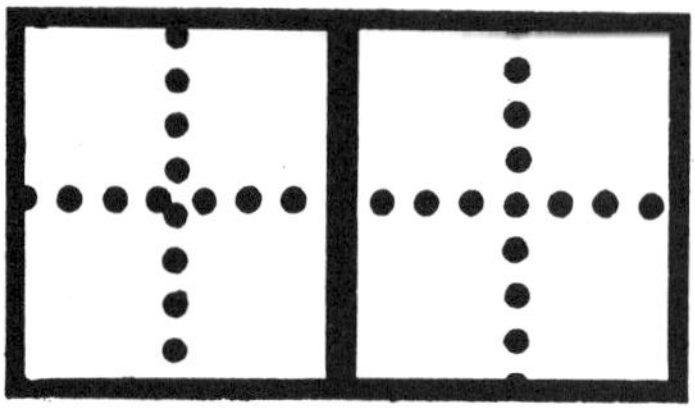

Automatic Machine Perforation. Stamps with unusual perforations, intended for use in automatic stamp-vending machines in the United States and elsewhere.
Illustrations: P103, 104, USA; P105, New Zealand.

Blind Perforation. A term applied to perforations where the holes are not punched out, due to blunt or missing perforating pins which leave the paper depressed or unmarked.
Illustrations: P106, Samoa; P107, USA.

Clean-cut Perforations. The ideal condition—where the holes are clean and the punched paper removed.
Illustration: P108, GB King Edward VIII, comb perforation.

Comb Perforation. So-called because the perforating pins are arranged in the form of a 'comb'—a long line of pins with a number of shorter lines at right-angles so that the top and sides of a row—or two, three or four rows—are perforated at a time. Usually identified by the evenness and regularity of the intersecting holes.
Illustration: P109, New Zealand, King Edward VII.

Compound Perforation. A term indicating the use of two or more different perforation gauges or measurements on the one stamp. Many stamps have the horizontal perforations in one gauge and the side (vertical) perforations in a different gauge, the horizontal measure usually given first, e.g. 'perf. $12\frac{1}{2} \times 14$'.
Illustrations: P110, Canada, perf 12×8; P112, Bosnia and Herzegovina, perf. $12\frac{1}{2}$, $9\frac{1}{2}$ and $6\frac{1}{2}$ compound.

Harrow Perforation. A means of perforating whole sheets at a time, the pins being arranged crosswise, rather like a honeycomb.
Illustration: P111, Austria perf. $10\frac{1}{2}$ harrow.

Imitation Perforation. Simulated perforations *printed* on the stamp. The first issue of Sirmoor, when reprinted in 1891, was copied, with perforations, from a dealer's catalogue.
Illustrations: P113, Sirmoor; P114, Obock.

Intermediate Perforation. A term applied specifically to Perkins Bacon printings of the 1860s in which perforations produced by a certain machine gradually deteriorated from the original 'clean-cut' to 'intermediate' and 'rough'.
Illustration: P120, St. Vincent.

Interrupted Perforation. A means of strengthening strips of stamps used in automatic vending machines, where gaps were created in the line of perforations by the omission of certain pins. Used by Holland, Danzig and other countries.
Illustrations: P115, 116, Netherlands; P117, Danzig.

P108

P109

P110

P111

P112

P113

P114

P115

P116

P117

P118

P120

P121

P122

P119

P123

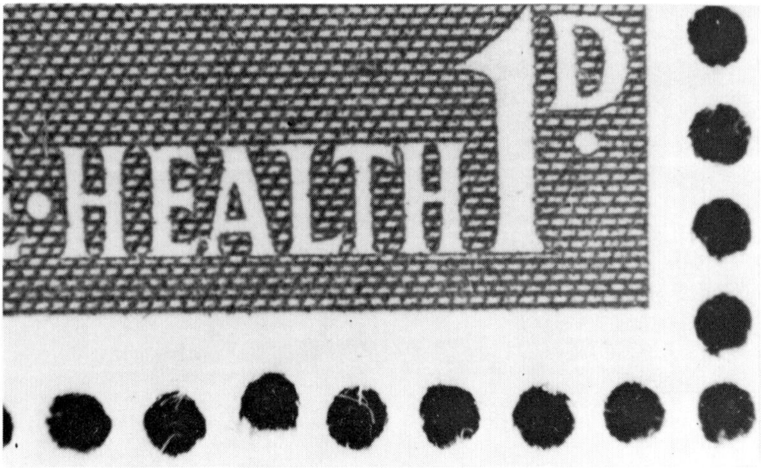

Irregular perforation on a New Zealand Health stamp

Irregular Perforation. Perforations out of alignment or of mixed measurement in one or more lines or sides of a stamp.
Illustration: P118, Mexico.

Line Perforation. The simplest form of perforation in which rows of stamps are punched in 'single lines', the sheets then being turned sideways-on and the process repeated. Line-perforated stamps can usually be identified by the fact that the intersecting holes at the corners of the stamps never—or rarely—precisely match.

Mixed Perforation. Stamps defectively perforated which have been patched on their backs and re-perforated, usually resulting in compound perfs. Notable examples are the New Zealand issues of 1901.
Illustration: P119, New Zealand.

Private Perforation. Unofficial perforations applied by private individuals or organisations before perforation methods had been generally adopted. Susse Frères of Paris perforated the current French stamps in 1861, making large holes about gauge 7, while Greek stamps of 1889–95 may be found perforated $8\frac{1}{2} \times 9\frac{1}{4}$ by the postmaster at Astakos, or pin-rouletted by the postmaster at Amphissa.
Illustrations: P121, Greece (Astakos); P122, France (Susse); P123, Greece (Amphissa).

Australia 'large and small' perforation holes

Rotary Perforation. A method of perforation which involved the use of toothed perforating wheels operating on the same principle as the normal line perforator, i.e. in one direction across the sheet of stamps, then crosswise.
Illustration: P124, US 1 c. Franklin.

Rough Perforation. The antithesis of 'clean-cut' perforation—holes with rough edges, imperfectly cut or punched, possibly with bits of paper adhering.
Illustrations: P125, Morvi (Indian) State; P126, Colombia (Antioquia) 'too late' stamp; P127, Jaipur (Indian) State.

Sewing-machine Perforation. In some countries where perforating machines were not available, ordinary sewing-machines were used to produce a crude type of perforation. As the paper was merely pricked by the needle, without any of it being cut out or removed, the result was really a 'pin roulette'.
Illustration: P128, Turkey.

Various Perforations. Besides those already mentioned, numerous varieties of perforation exist on stamps, many of a freakish nature. Certain early stamps of Queensland were perforated by square holes in combination with round holes *and* pin roulette, while the first Bulgarian postage due stamps were perforated by lozenge-shaped holes. Some Australian stamps have a special coil perforation of large and small holes, intended to facilitate separation when withdrawing the stamps from vending machines. Some modern stamps of Mexico also have alternate large and small holes, and the first issues of Bussahir have large holes, gauging between 7 and 11½, made by a type of fitted sewing-machine.
Illustrations: P129, Bussahir (Indian) State; P130, Queensland 'combination' perforation; P131, Bulgaria 'lozenge' or diamond-shaped perforation; P132, Mexico.

P124

P125

P126

P127

P128

P129

P130

P131

P132

P133

P134

P135

P136

P137

P138

P139

Perforation—Rouletting. The word 'roulette' is taken from the French: it is literally a tool with a toothed disc or wheel for perforating paper, etc. While, however, cuts are made in the paper, no portion of it is removed. In philately, the various kinds of roulette are also given French terms, preceded by the word 'percé' ('pierced'). Rouletting is performed by a hand-tool or, in modern production, by a machine.

Arc Roulette (*Percé en arc.*) Curved cuts which appear as scalloped edges on the stamps. Also sometimes described as serrated roulette. *Illustration: P133, Brunswick.*

Compound Roulette. A convenient term indicating that the guage or type of roulette is not consistent on all four sides of the stamp. *Illustrations: P134, Yugoslavia 'Chainbreakers'—zigzag × straight roulettes; P135, Madagascar British Consular Mail—imperf top and bottom, roulette × arc roulette at sides.*

Diamond or Lozenge Roulette (*Percé en losanges*). Cuts in the form of tiny crosses, forming diamonds or lozenges with open corners. Unusual and rare. Also known as *Percé en croix.*

Experimental Roulette. Trial perforations, such as the experimental roulette 12 used by Henry Archer on GB Penny Reds of 1841, also known as 'Archer perforation' or 'Archer roulette'. The first issues of Madeira were experimentally rouletted (*P136*), the basic stamps being the Portuguese 'embossed' imperforates of 1866–7.

Oblique Roulette (*Percé en lignes obliques*). A rare type of roulette in which the cuts are aslant and parallel. Such stamps are not easily separated, and the edges of detached stamps are usually rough and irregular.
Illustration : P137, Van Diemen's Land.

Pin Roulette (*Percé en points*). This type of roulette consists of a series of holes pricked in the paper which, however, is not removed from the holes as in 'pin perforation'.
Illustrations : P138, Mexico 'square pin' roulette ; P139, Kishangarh (*Indian*) *State.*

Roulette (Percé en lignes)

Roulette (*Percé en lignes*). The 'normal', basic roulette comprising straight cuts. The measure of their separation provides numerous varieties.
Illustrations : P140, Portuguese India, cut with toothed strips of ivory ; P141, Chile 'Columbus' ; P142, Mexico 'Eagle'.

Roulette in Colour (*Percé en lignes de couleur*). An unusual form of roulette which is produced at the time of printing—notched rules placed between the cliches forming the plate are inked at the same time as the plate, and in the course of printing the rouletted cuts or slits have coloured edges.
Illustrations : P143, Queensland 'Penny Red' (*rouletted in black after printing*) *; P144, Thurn and Taxis, Northern District ; P145, Kishangarh* (*Indian*) *State.*

P140

P141

P142

P143

P144

P145

P148

P146

P147

P149

P150

P151

P152

P153

P154

P155

P156

P157

Saw-tooth Roulette (*Percé en scie*). Cuts made in a zigzag line and, when the stamps are separated, having the appearance of the teeth of a saw—forerunner of the modern zigzag roulette.
Illustration : P146, La Guaira (Venezuela) local 'packet' post.

Serpentine Roulette (*Percé en serpentine*). 'Old fashioned' style of roulette in which cuts in the form of wavy lines are made between the stamps, the lines being interrupted in the centre of each 'wave' to prevent the sheets from disintegration. When the stamps are separated, the uncut portion appears in the form of a small 'shoulder'. Sometimes erroneously termed 'serpentine perforation'.
Illustrations : P147, 148, Finland local posts ; P149, Finland 1860.

Serrated Roulette. Small, semi-circular cuts, in fact a very fine variety of the 'arc roulette'. 'Serrated perforation' is a misnomer.
Illustration : P150, Van Diemen's Land.

Zigzag Roulette

Zigzag Roulette (*Percé en pointes*). A roulette in which the cuts produce sharp points along the edges of the stamps, the effect being similar to that of the 'saw-tooth roulette', though the points are smaller.
Illustrations: P151, Germany 'inflation' stamps; P152, Greece; P153, Danzig air stamp.

Compound of Perforation and Roulette. During World War II, when the (then) Union of South Africa reduced the size of her postage stamps in order to economise in the use of paper, it was found expedient to alter the perforating machines to accommodate the new 'bantam' size by an alternate arrangement of perforation and rouletting. The perforations allowed separation into pairs, blocks or units of stamps, rouletting permitted easier separation of single stamps. A compound of perforation and coloured roulette was used on a $\frac{1}{4}$ anna stamp of Duttia (India) about 1912, and certain stamps issued in Queensland in 1899 can be found with perforation and roulette together, on the same stamp.
Illustrations: P154, 155, South African 'bantams'; P156, Duttia; P157, Queensland.

Phosphor. The popular name for stamps overprinted, inked or impregnated with phosphorescent or 'fluorescent' substances for use in electronic letter-facing and postmarking machines. Such stamps (also described as 'luminescent' because they emit light) on letters react or 'fluoresce', i.e. emit rays of a certain wavelength when subjected to radiation under ultra-violet lamps. The resulting glow of the phosphorescent ink is 'seen' by the scanner, which separates first and second class mail.

The British Post Office introduced automatic letter-facing in 1957 with experimental stamps having black graphite lines printed on the back. Translucent phosphor bands were introduced in 1958 and have continued in use to the present day. All British stamps except the high values (£1 upwards) are now phosphor-banded—usually two vertical bands for first-class mail, one band for second-class or, for special or commemorative stamps for first-class mail (single-banded, second class), coated overall phosphor. The bands are not easily visible, except when the stamps are viewed against the light with the eye almost level with the face or surface. Certain definitives have been issued experimentally with overall phosphor (coated on the printed stamps), while the 'Racket Sports' issue of 1977 was printed on phosphor-coated paper.

Illustrations: P158, GB 4½d. two band definitive: P159, GB 1s. 3d. three-band commemorative.

Phosphor bands applied by typography (left) and by photogravure (right)

P158

P159

P160

P161

P162

P163

P164

P165

P166

P167

P168

P169

P170

P171

P172

P173

P174

P175

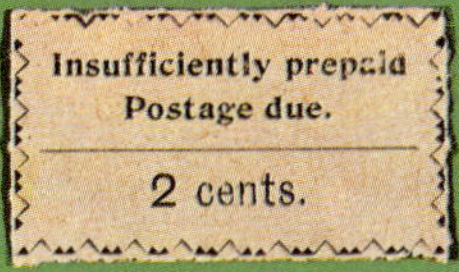

P176

P177

P178

P179

P180

P181

P182

P183

P184

P185

P186

P187

P188

P189

Plate-numbers. Numerals and/or letters inscribed on sheets of stamps, usually in the margins at the foot or sides, indicating the plate or plates used in printing the stamps on a flat-bed press (as opposed to a rotary press—see 'Cylinder-numbers'). Some plates are divided into two, three or four panes of stamps, each pane having an identifying letter, as for example, plates '1, 1A, 1B, 1C'. The stamps of Great Britain from 1858 to 1880 bore the plate-numbers within the framework of the stamps themselves, as well as in the margins of the sheets.
Illustrations: P160, GB Penny Red with number (193) in the borders (both sides); P161, Ceylon plate 2; P162, Hong Kong plates 1 *(blue), 1 (brown).*

Plebiscite Stamps. Stamps issued by temporarily independent states while their future nationality or political affinity is decided by plebiscite or referendum, i.e. popular vote.
Illustrations: P163, Schleswig; P164, P166, Allenstein: P165, Slovenia; P167, Peru.

Plug. Literally a part of a stamp printing-plate, inserted or plugged into the main design. Examples are found in the early stamps of Haiti which were all printed from the same plate, the various figures of value being plugged in as required. A similar method is used to repair damaged plates.
Illustration: P169, Haiti 5c.

Pneumatic Post. A system of conveying letters by underground pneumatic tubes, used principally in the larger towns of France and Italy. Special fees were charged for the service, and in the case of Italy, stamps inscribed 'Posta Pneumatica' were issued between 1913 and 1966 for the inter-post office pneumatic services operating in Rome, Milan, Naples, Turin and Genoa.
Illustrations: P168, P170

Post Offices Abroad. Post Offices staffed and operated by one country, located 'by favour' in another country, international zone, concession or occupied territory, and using appropriately inscribed or surcharged stamps. Examples are the former British Post Offices in the Gulf States of Bahrain, Kuwait and Muscat, etc., China, Morocco (Agencies and Tangier), Crete and Thailand (Bangkok); and the French, German and Italian Post Offices in various parts of the world.
Illustrations: P171, German P.O. in China and, P173, Morocco; P172, British P.O. in Tangier (International Zone) and, P174, Morocco.

Postage Due Stamps. Used by the post office to denote the sums to be collected on delivery of unstamped letters, or those which are insufficiently prepaid or stamped for the correct postal rate. They are affixed to the letters by the postal staff, the due sum—which may be double the amount of the deficiency—being collected by the postman from the addressee on delivery. Not on general sale to the public, but usually supplied in unused condition through philatelic bureaux. Most countries of the world use postage due stamps or alternatively the hand-stamped letter 'T', representing the French word 'taxe'.,

British postage due stamps were first introduced in 1914 and remained unchanged in design until 1970. The higher values were inscribed 'TO Pay' as they were extensively used for the collection of customs' duties on packages and parcels from abroad. The new decimal-currency postage dues issued in 1970–71 are *all* inscribed 'TO PAY'. The dues of France and French-language countries are inscribed 'à payer', 'à percevoir', or 'timbre taxe'; several countries including Denmark, Hungary and Yugoslavia, 'porto'; Netherlands, 'te betalen port'; Italy, 'segnatasse'; Portugal, 'porteado' or 'a cobrar' (to collect).
Illustrations: P175, P177, Old and new British postage due stamps; P176, Zanzibar, 1930; P178, Canada; P179, Denmark military post; P180 Trinidad postage'; P181, South Africa; P182, Tunisia perforated 'T'.

International Reply Coupon

P190

P191

P192

P193

P194

P195

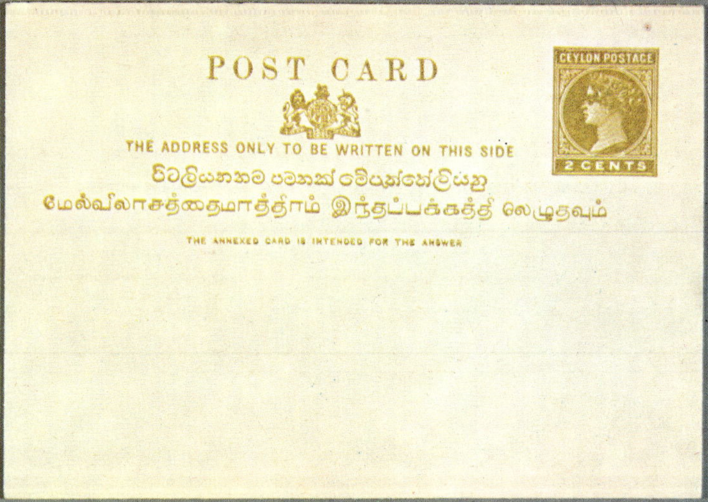

P196

P197

P198

P199

P200

P201

P202

Postal Currency. In early days the Treasury of the United States issued small tokens or coupons in order to provide facilities for transferring small sums of money by post, and these were accepted by the Post Office in exchange for postage stamps.
Illustration: P183.

International Reply Coupons. Issued by country members of the Universal Postal Union to provide a convenient method for sending reply postage with letters. The coupons are exchanged for postage stamps by the post office in the destination country.

Postal Fiscals. Fiscal or revenue stamps authorised for postal use. Many postage stamps also have fiscal use and are usually inscribed 'Postage and Revenue'.
Illustrations: P184, Dominica; P185, Hong Kong (used in Shanghai); P186, Colombia; P187, Western Australia; P188, Victoria; P189, New Zealand.

Postal Stationery. All forms of postal envelopes, cards, wrappers etc. which have impressed or imprinted stamps.

Cut Square. Imprinted stamp cut from envelope, card etc. in the form of a square or rectangle.
Illustrations; P190, GB card; P191, Egypt; P192, GB envelope.

Cut to Shape. As above, but items cut to outline of stamp design.
Illustrations: P193/195, GB envelopes.

Letter Cards. 'Double' postcards which can be folded and sealed. Liable to letter rate.

Registered Envelope. Special envelope for use by registered mail.

Reply Paid Cards. Joined pair of prepaid postal cards, one being detachable for the reply.
Illustration: P196, Ceylon.

Superimposed Adhesives. Ordinary stamps affixed over imprinted stamps on postal stationery by the North German Federation in 1868 for various member states. A protective burélage was embossed partly on the stamp and partly on the cover.
Illustrations: P197, P198.

Postcard Stamp. In the Orange Free State, adhesive stamps were affixed to postcards and overprinted with the State arms and sometimes additionally surcharged.
Illustration: P199.

Used as Adhesive. A practice accepted by most post offices of the world is that of cutting out the imprinted stamps on postal stationery items and affixing them to envelopes etc. for postal use.
Illustrations: P200, GB postcard 'stamp'; P201, Ecuador wrapper 'stamps'; P202, Prussia envelope 'stamp'.

Early GB postmark

Postal Telegraphs. Stamps originally issued for use on telegrams, subsequently permitted, provisionally or permanently, to be used as postage stamps. As, however, telegraphic cancellations are often very similar to normal postmarks, it is sometimes impossible to say with certainty which stamps have been genuinely used for postal purposes. Examples are the overprinted telegraph stamps of Orange Free State. *Illustrations: P203, Argentine Republic; P204, Chile; P205, Western Australia.*

Postal Union Colours. A Washington convention of the Universal Postal Union in 1898 recommended that the stamps of its member countries should be uniformly and distinctively coloured, primarily for the three most-used denominations, i.e. green, red and blue respectively, for printed matter, postcards and 'single rate' letters in the international postal services. Most countries adopted the ruling which held good for more than 50 years, but the disruption of currencies and disparity of postage rates following World War II led to the abandonment of the scheme in 1953.
Illustrations: P206/8, GB King Edward VII; P209/11, France; P212/4, United States.

Postcard Tax Stamp. Stamps of Persia overprinted 'Controle', issued in 1904, were used to levy a tax on picture postcards sent through the post, and had to be affixed to the cards in addition to the usual postal charge.
Illustrations: P215/6.

Postmark. Any mark, handstruck, machine-applied or in manuscript form, used on postal items in order to cancel the stamps and/or record the date and origin of their transit through the mail service, whereas a 'cancellation' (q.v.) is *any* kind of defacing mark on a stamp (including 'postmark'). An 'obliteration' is a mark specifically employed in defacing or obliterating stamps i.e. a form of cancellation.

There is an infinite variety in the designs of postmarks, especially of the early types, ranging from the 'pre-adhesive' handstruck marks of Bishop and Dockwra etc., code letters, numbers and devices, town and street names to the modern commemorative and slogan marks. Postmarks are an essential ingredient in the postal history 'pie', and indeed many a 'plum' in a specialised collection will be in the form of

P203

P206

P207

P208

P204

P209

P210

P211

P205

P212

P213

P214

P215

P216

P217

P218

P219

P220

P221

P222

P223

P224

P225

P226

P227

P229

P228

P230

a distinctive (and possibly rare) postal cancellation.

For various reasons postmarks have an especial attraction for many collectors. Legible, dated postmarks on stamps help to identify particular issues, their origin and period of use. In the last century British stamps were used in the Colonies before they had their own stamps, and often such stamps 'used abroad' in this way may only be identified by the postmark. French stamps postmarked with numerals within a diamond pattern may have been used in one or other of the many French overseas post offices or agencies. Ideally, in cases where the postmark is of greater interest or value than the stamp, the original envelope or cover should be preserved.

Some people collect the postmarks of their own home town, suburb or county, combining them with studies of local postal history. Others specialise in railway or 'travelling post office' cancellations, or the 'paquebot' marks used aboard ships at sea, or on mail received from ships. Modern slogan and pictorial cancellations are sometimes very attractive and often hold thematic interest for the collector of birds, buildings, flowers etc. These are best collected 'on piece', a section approximately $4 \times 1\frac{1}{2}$ inches (or larger, according to the size and shape of the postmark), allowing a fair margin on all sides of the actual mark, being neatly cut from the envelope or wrapper.

Illustrations: P217/8, Glasgow postmarks of 1869 and 1940; P219, London machine-cancellation of King George V's reign; P220/3, Numeral cancellations of GB, Victoria and France; P224, Modern machine cancellation which is also a commemorative or 'slogan' mark.

Backstamp. Postmarks applied to the backs of letters for the purpose of recording the time, date and place of arrival, or points *en route*. Now used principally on registered mail and (in this country) on letters from abroad.

Commemorative. Special postmark used to commemorate exhibitions, conferences, international sports meetings, anniversaries and notable events of all kinds. Often collected in conjunction with the stamps issued for the same occasion. Among the earliest commemorative postmarks were those used during the British Empire Exhibition at Wembley, 1924–25.

Illustrations: P225, GB, Philatelic Congress of Great Britain, Cambridge, 1938; P226, GB Arrival of Gurkha Brigade Contingent, Aldershot, 1971; P227, East Germany, Durer's 500th birth anniversary (and stamps), 1971.

Christmas. From 1902 to 1909, the British Post Office endeavoured to relieve pressure on postal staff in the days before Christmas by introducing an advance postage scheme. In certain towns, letters

Letter backstamped at point of dispatch (Ringwood, Hants) and on arrival at Dar-es-Salaam (now in Tanzania)

intended for delivery on Christmas Day could be handed in at a post office up to a specified day. Various types of special postmarks were issued during the period the service was in use.
Illustration: P228, GB, Manchester, 1906.

Deferential. Postmarks so designed that when a stamp was cancelled, the effigy of the reigning monarch was not defaced, notably in Sicily and Spain. For the antithesis of this practice (stamp portraits barred or blotted-out), see 'Obliterated Stamps'.
Illustrations: P229, Bhor (Indian State); P230, Sicily.

Duplex. The first combined two-part cancellation and datestamp, called, from its dual purpose, a 'duplex mark'. The heavily-barred, oval obliteration which usually formed the 'cancellation' part was also known as a 'killer' (q.v.).
Illustrations: P231, Birmingham duplex; P232, Edinburgh type.

First Day. Commemorative postmark used (usually in conjunction with special envelopes) on the first day of issue of new stamps.
Illustrations: P233, Liechtenstein; P234, Algeria.

P231

P232

P233

P234

P235

P236

P237

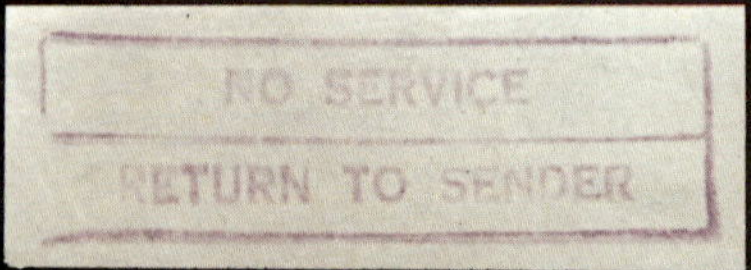

P238

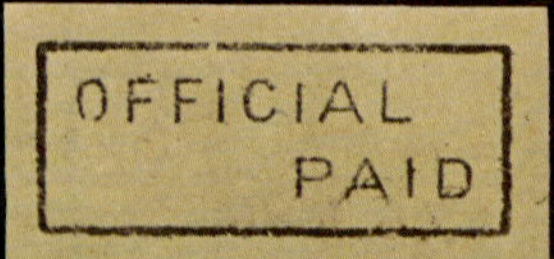

P239

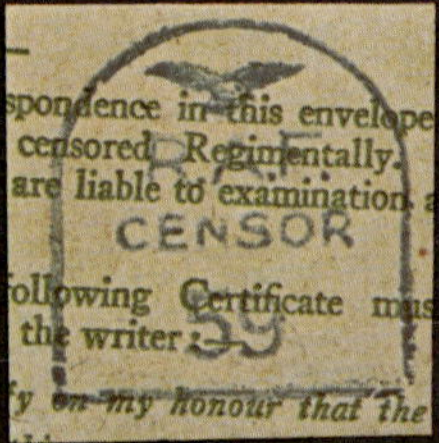

P240

P241

P242

P243

P244

P245

P246

P247

P248

P249

P250

Informative. Types of postmark indicating fees paid or to be collected, censorship, non-delivery and similar information of service to postal officials and the public.
Illustrations: P235/6, 'To Pay' marks; P237, Liverpool 'Paid' mark of 1847; P238, Non-delivery; P239, Official 'Paid'; P240, RAF Censor's mark.

'Killer'. Early form of obliteration consisting of heavy bars, cork impressions and other crude devices.
Illustrations: P241/2, US 'Killers'.

Machine Cancellation. A postmark applied by an automatic machine as opposed to handstamping, typified in Britain by a wavy-line pattern adjoining the date stamp where no slogan is used.
See illustrations P219, P224.

Maltese Cross. The first cancellation or obliteration used on British stamps, 1840–44, derived its name partly from its shape and partly from the badge of the Knights of Malta, which it resembles. At first the Crosses were red; later, when the 'Penny Reds' were introduced, it was changed to black. Other colours are known.
Illustrations: P243/4.

Manuscript. Emergency cancellation by pen and ink. Also 'Pen Cancelled'.

Wartime manuscript cancellation used in the Gilbert & Ellice Islands

Mutilation. Early Afghan stamps were 'cancelled' by having a small portion cut or torn off.
Illustration: P245.

Paquebot. ('Packet Boat'). Term given to letters posted on board ships at sea and to the form of postmark invariably used.
Illustrations: P246, Royal Navy wartime mark; P247/50, 'Paquebot' marks used on stamps of Dominica, Nicaragua, Bahamas and GB.

'Registered' postmark

Parcel Post. The Parcel Post was inaugurated in the United Kingdom in 1883, and since then many distinctive types of postmark have been used, ranging from the Victorian 'roller' cancellation to the large contemporary rectangles. Comparatively rare examples of commemorative parcel postmarks were those used at the British Empire Exhibition at Wembley in 1924–25.
Illustrations: P251, Manchester roller cancellation; P252, Present-day cancellation.

Printed Matter. Numerous types of postmark have been used (a) to cancel circulars and other commercial printed matter, and (b) to indicate special rates of postage for newspapers.
Illustrations: P253, 'Dublin Gazette' 1d. newspaper 'paid' stamp; P254, Glasgow 'NPB' ('Newspaper Branch') mark; P255, Manchester 'paid' stamp.

Registered Post. Special postmarks which indicate that a letter or packet has been accepted (and an extra fee paid) for conveyance by registered post. In early days a 'killer' cancellation consisting of a large letter 'R' within an oval or circle was used in addition to the normal datestamp by various countries, notably the Australian States and Canada.
Illustrations: P256, Auckland (New Zealand) 'Registered' cancellation; P257, Present-day GB oval 'Registered' mark.

Services Postmarks. Used by the armed forces at peacetime stations at home and abroad, in time of war or on manoeuvres. The British services currently use 'Field Post Office' circular datestamps which are identified only by the office number within the postmark, a precaution against revealing the field location of a particular regiment or unit. Examples of wartime usage are the special field postmarks used by British forces in South Africa during the Boer War, and by General Northey's Nyasa-Rhodesian Force (on special overprinted 'NF' stamps) in conquered territory of German East Africa during World War I.
Illustrations: P258, US Army Post Office No. 506 mark with 'Killer' bars; P259 GB Field Post Office No. 895 mark; P260, US Army Air Force (combined) A.P.O. No. 09676 mark.

P251

P252

P253

P254

P255

P256

P257

P258

P259

P260

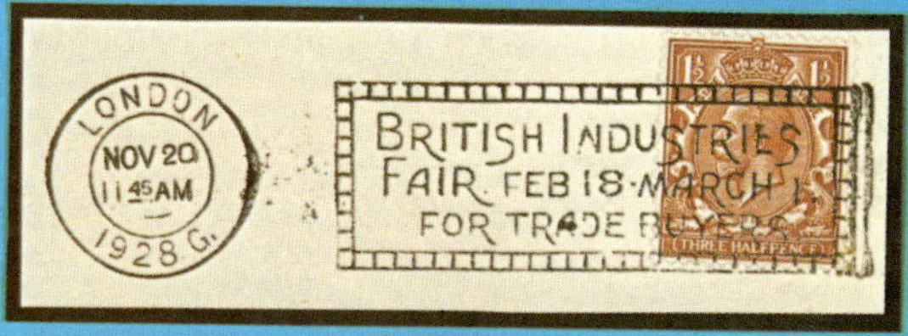

P261

P262

P263

P264

P265

Slogan Postmarks. A comparatively modern form of postmarking which is, in fact, a mechanical development of the old-time duplex handstamp, comprising official slogans or advertising catch-phrases. The first British postmark slogan—perhaps the first in the world, exhorted the public to 'Buy National War Bonds Now', and was introduced during World War I. At first, British slogan marks were confined to Government announcements, such as the ubiquitous 'Post Early for Christmas'.

Now, the Post Office caters for all kinds of public causes and events, the cost of the postmarks being borne by the respective sponsors. A popular form of modern slogan is the pictorial 'holiday resort' postmark. Pictorial postmarks are a very popular field, especially those of Britain, France and Switzerland which are sought by thematic collectors to illustrate their particular stamp themes.

Illustrations: P261, GB 'British Industries Fair', 1928; P262, GB 'Save St Paul's', 1971.

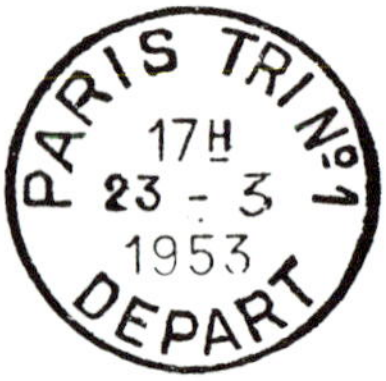

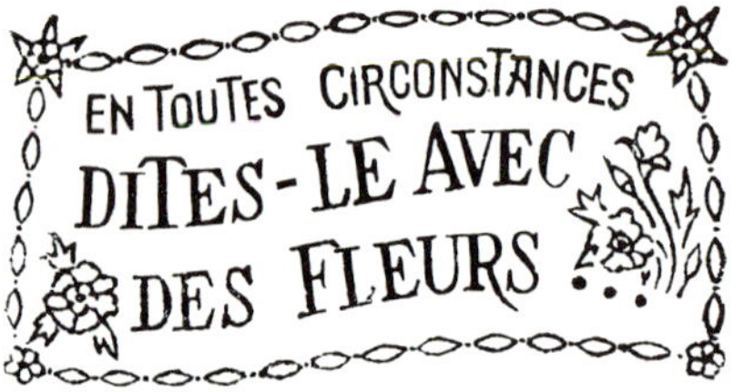

Town Circles. The first GB 'town name' postmarks succeeded the Maltese Crosses in about 1842, and these were followed by the duplex, the so-called 'spoon', 'squared circle' and other variations. The modern town c.d.s. (circular date-stamp) or handstamp is used in smaller towns and post offices where there are no facilities for machine cancellation. They are extremely popular with collectors of GB and Commonwealth stamps.

Illustration: P263, Devoran, Truro c.d.s.

Travelling Post Offices. Postmarks used on mail which has been sorted aboard special postal railway coaches or trains, and which may have been picked up and/or delivered at selected points *en route.* Such postmarks may be identified by the letters 'T.P.O.' and the route, 'Cardiff–Crewe T.P.O.', also 'R.P.O.' ('Railway Post Office') especially in Canada, 'M.C.' ('Mail Carriage') or 'S.T.' ('Sorting Tender'). An unusual postmark is the rail/ship 'M.B.' c.d.s.—'Boîte Mobile' or 'Movable Box', a kind of portable postbox used on Channel crossings.
Illustrations: P264, France–Southampton 'M.B.' mark; P265, US Royal Train R.P.O.

Swiss Alpine postal coaches of 1909 and 1949

Precancelled Stamps. Intended for business organisations posting circulars in bulk—stamps issued precancelled or postmarked in advance usually bearing the town name or code numerals, used especially in Canada and the US.
Illustrations: P266, US; P267, Belgium; P268, France; P269, Canada; P270, Luxembourg.

Premières Gravures. The name given to the first issue of US 1861 'Presidents' stamps, the designs being subsequently amended.
Illustrations: P271, Original 3 c; P272, Amended 3 c. with addition of 'ball' in each corner.

Printed Matter Stamps. Specially issued for the prepayment of postage on printed matter, circulars etc.
Illustrations: P273, Spanish Philippines; P274, Czechoslovakia 'O.T.' ('Obchodni Tiskovina').

Printed on Back. Numerous stamps may be found with printing of some sort on the back—captions or slogans, control or series numbers, figures of value, even surcharges and 'watermarks'. Portugal issued stamps in 1895 for St Anthony of Padua with a Latin prayer printed on the back. 'Pears Soap' appeared on the back of certain GB stamps issued in 1887, and various advertisements on New Zealand stamps *circa* 1893.
Illustrations: P275, Fiume postal slogan; P276, Mauritius 'tourist' slogan; P277, Hungary charity premium.

P266

P267

P268

P269

P270

P271

P272

P273

P274

P275

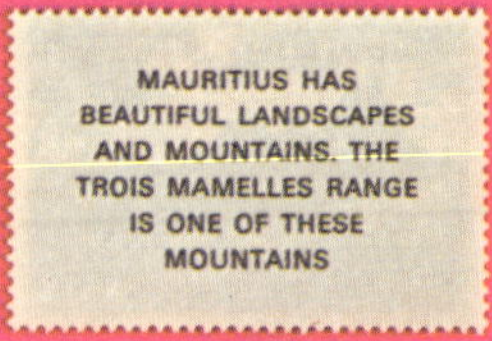

P276

P277

P278

P279

P280

P281

P282

P283

P284

P286

P287

P285

P288

P289

P290

P291

P292

P293

P294

P295

P296

P297

P298

P299

P300

P301

P302

P303

Printer's Type. The many different styles and sizes of printer's types used on stamps are of interest to philatelists. The various type-faces have distinctive characteristics, and they are used in the actual printed stamp or in the form of an overprint.

Fancy. A general term covering the many decorative styles of type which do not conform to regular founts.
Illustrations: P280, Niger Oil Rivers Protectorate 'Half Penny'; P281, Natal 'Half'; P282, New Caledonia 'N.C.E.' (shaded type) and '5 c.'; P283, Costa Rica '2 cts.'.

German. Also 'Gothic' or 'Old English'—a heavy, decorative and rather elaborate type.
Illustrations: P284, Germany, China Post Offices; P285, Shanghai postage due; P286, Bavaria; P287, St Pierre and Miquelon 'SPM'; P288, Netherlands 'Veertig Cent' (40 c.) on 30 c.

Italic. A type with sloping letters, used chiefly for emphasis.
Illustrations: P289, Sungei Ujong; P290, Tasmania 'ONE PENNY'; P291, Memel 5 pfennig.

Roman. The type, distinguished by its capital letters having serifs or short cross-lines at the end of the strokes, most used in general printing.
Illustrations: P292, Trinidad & Tobago 'War Tax'; P293, Costa Rica 'OFICIAL'; P294, Uganda Protectorate; P295, Angola 'REPUBLICA'; P296, Sungei Ujong.

Sans-serif. Styles of type in which the capital letters are without serifs.
Illustrations: P297, Tonga 'FIVE PENCE'; P298, North Borneo 'WAR TAX'; P299, Bahamas 'SPECIAL DELIVERY'; P300, Sungei Ujong.

Mixed Founts. In Victorian times, it was considered a sign of good printing to use as many founts of type as possible, and as many as 14 are known to have been used on a printed page. Mixed founts have often been used for type-set stamps and overprints.
Illustrations: P301, Perak; P302, Sonora, Mexico; P303, Selangor.

Printer's Waste. Any defective, malformed or misprinted stamps which are normally discarded and burned by the printer.
Illustrations: P278, Spain 1874—lemon-yellow of 2 c. misapplied (and inverted) on 5 c. mauve; P279, Montenegro 1896, misprinted and 'blue-pencilled'.

GB 10d. and 1s. 'Embossed' of 1847–48

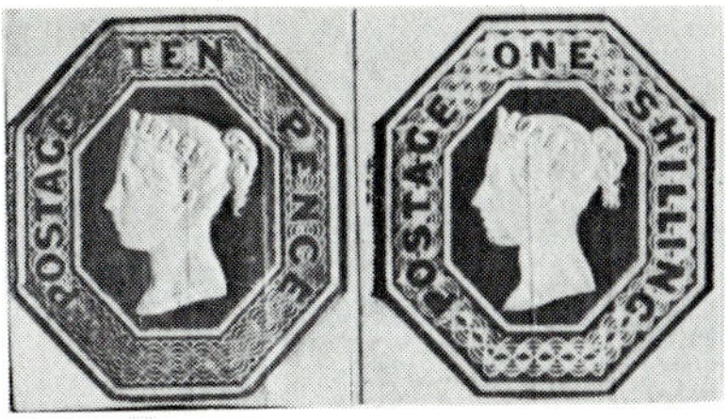

Printing Processes and Terms

Several processes have been used for printing postage stamps—some have 'fallen by the wayside' and there are now three principal methods by which stamps are printed and produced. These are line-engraving (or 'recess'), lithography and photogravure. Typography (letterpress or 'surface-printing') is on the decline for printing stamps, while embossing or 'die-stamping' is enjoying a limited vogue, particularly in coloured relief on gold and similar metallic foils, in certain countries catering for the philatelic market. The standards of stamp printing have reached a high level of quality which, however, is closely related to costs. The craftsman engravers are gradually being ousted by more complex processes and more sophisticated printing machines.

Collotype. Or collotypy. A form of gelatine process used principally in book illustration and advertising, similar to photogravure but without screening and other gravure refinements. The glass printing plate bears the image in shallow relief (in reverse), from which impressions are taken with suitable inks. Its main philatelic use was as a kind of photo-copier, and it has been the medium for some plausible forgeries.
Illustrations: Collotypic versions of: P304, Queensland; P305, New South Wales; P306, St Vincent.

Embossing. Or 'Die-stamping'. Strictly speaking, a method of stamping in relief rather than a printing process, though allied to print in the production of postage stamps and postal stationery. The relief or raised impression is obtained by placing the paper between two matching dies, one (male) bearing the design image in relief, the other having the (female) counterpart of the image in recess. The usual form of embossing is clear (or 'blind') as opposed to coloured (see introduction).
Illustrations: P307, Iceland; P308, Portuguese India; P309, Bavaria; P310, Gambia.

P304

P305

P306

P307

P308

P309

P310

P311

P312

P313

P314

P315

P316

P317

P318

P319

P320

P321

P322

P323

P324

P325

P326

P327

P328

P329

P330

P331

P332

P333

P334

P335

P336

P337

Engine-turning. A kind of ornamentation made by a rose-engine or lathe, which enables intricate geometrical patterns to be engraved mechanically on steel, used to form the 'unforgeable' backgrounds on banknotes and postage stamps. It was Jacob Perkins, an American, who adapted and improved the rose-engine, first used on the line-engraved stamps (Penny Black and Twopence Blue) printed by Perkins, Bacon and Petch in 1840.
Illustrations: P311, China; P312, New South Wales; P313, Mexico; P314, St Vincent.

Half-tone. A photo-mechanical method of representing light and shade by dots of varying size, extensively used for the reproduction of illustration blocks in newspapers and magazines. Akin to gravure in that the subject is photographed through a fine screen on a sensitised plate of copper or zinc and subsequently etched. Probably the cheapest reproductive medium and, for that reason, occasionally used in stamp production. Modern examples are the stamps of the Netherlands (definitives) and of Persia.
Illustrations: P315, Kishangarh; P316, Latvia; P317, Saudi Arabia.

Line Block. An illustration block produced in a similar fashion to a half-tone, but without the screen. In printing from line blocks (in conjunction with typography) only extreme contrast is possible, though graduated tones may be suggested by the use of lines of varying thickness.
Illustrations: P318, 320, New Zealand; P319, Turkey.

Line Engraving. Also 'recess', *taille-douce* (Fr.) or *intaglio* (It.). A process of engraving in lines *in recess* on steel or copperplate. This process was pioneered by Perkins Bacon, the printers of the first British (and world) postage stamps in 1840, and the traditional methods still apply today. The design image is cut on a steel or copper 'master die', in stamp size, in recess and in reverse, then the die is hardened and its image transferred to the comparatively soft steel surface of a cylinder or roller (the 'transfer roller') under pressure.

The roller's surface is then hardened and the design image again transferred, as many times as needed to form a sheet of maybe 60, 100 or 200 stamps, under close pressure (known as 'rocking in') onto the thin steel plate which will be used to print the stamps. At this stage, the plate, which may be used flat in a 'flatbed' press, or curved around a cylinder for printing in a 'rotary 'press, again has the design images in reverse so that the printed stamps will be the 'right way round'. Finally, ink is applied to the design recesses and printing proceeds while the press is in operation. An alternative method of obtaining multiple images is by electrotyping in which a plate is formed

of duplicate moulds of the original die.
Illustrations: P321, Norway; P322, British Guiana; P323, Netherlands; P324, Chile; P325, Liechtenstein; P326, Comoro Islands; P327, Russia.

Lithography. A method of surface-printing in which the design is laid down on the 'stone' or plate of zinc or some other metal such as aluminium, in greasy ink, or by means of 'transfers', in reverse. After 'fixing' by acid, the stone is continuously dampened in the course of printing—the printing ink adheres only to the greased image which has meanwhile repelled the water. A printed impression is obtained when paper is brought in contact with the stone or plate.
Illustrations: P328, Mexico; P329, Syria; P330, Venezuela; P331, Greece.
In modern offset (photo-) lithography, the design is photographed onto a flexible zinc or aluminium plate which, after processing, is curved around a cylinder for use in a rotary press. The revolving, inked cylinder is brought in close contact with a 'blanket' roller which receives a reversed impression of the original plate of stamp images. These are transferred in turn by 'offset' contact with the paper which is fed by the 'impression' cylinder. A special photo-litho process involving the use of fine screens—known as 'Delacryl'—is used by De La Rue.
Illustrations: P332, Chile; P333, China (Formosa); P334, Dubai; P335, Finland; P336, Turks & Caicos Islands; P337, Argentine Republic.

Mixed Printing. For various reasons, individual stamps have been produced by more than one printing process. Sometimes parts of a design will reproduce better in another style or type of printing.
Illustrations: P362, Chile (head engraved, frame litho); P363, Uruguay (vignette half-tone, frame line-block); P364, Chile (head litho, frame typo.); P365, Czechoslovakia; P368, Russia; P371, Belgium—all recess and photo; P366, 369, USA; P370, South Viet-Nam—all recess and litho; P367, Poland, recess and typo.

Photography. Examples of stamps produced solely by photography occurred during the Siege of Mafeking in 1900, when 1d. and 3d. stamps were locally printed and issued. Glass negatives were prepared from drawings and photographs, and printing was effected by the ferro-prussiate process commonly used in the production of blueprints.
Illustration: P338, Mafeking 1d.

Photogravure. Also 'gravure' (in the printing world) and 'roto-gravure' (American origin, meaning 'rotary gravure'). A form of recess printing. The basic design is photographed and the negative is used as a kind of 'master die' from which a series of positive images (as many as required to form a sheet of stamps) is produced on a glass plate —the 'multipositive'. The plate is processed upon a carbon tissue which

P338

P339

P340

P341

P342

P343

P344

P345

P346

P347

P348

P349

P350

P351

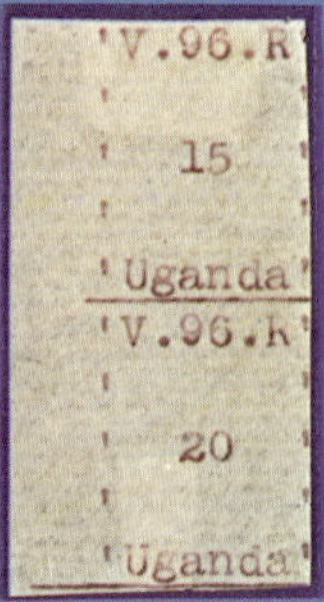

P352

P353

P354

P355

P356

P357

P358

P359

P360

P361

P362

P363

P364

P365

P366

P367

P368

P369

P370

P371

has a 'screened' surface—a fine network of criss-cross lines. Next the carbon tissue is wrapped around a copper cylinder and etched with a solution of ferric chloride, leaving a pattern of small cells or recesses (corresponding to the 'grid' formation of the screen) on the cylinder—these vary in depth according to the strength of tone in the multipositive images. The cylinder is then chromium-plated and prepared for printing.
Illustrations: P339, Egypt; P340, Luxembourg; P341, GB; P342, Netherlands Antilles; P343, Cook Islands; P344, Papua and New Guinea; P345, Australia; P346, Hungary; P347, China (Formosa).

Stereotype. A solid metallic plate for printing, cast from a plastic mould of movable types. The Cape of Good Hope 'Woodblocks' were engraved on steel and printed from stereotyped plates.

Thermoplastics. A process of plastic-surfacing used, in conjunction with lithography, by Turkey. Bhutan stamps have laminated prismatic-ribbed plastic surfaces which provide three-dimensional effects.

Type-set. Made up from movable types.
Illustrations: P348, Guadeloupe; P349, Madagascar; P350, Surinam; P351, Malta.

Typewriting. The most simple form of philatelic typography. Typewritten stamps were produced by the Rev. E. Miller in Uganda in 1895, and similar provisional stamps were used during the British occupation of Long Island (Aegean Sea) in 1916.
Illustrations: P352, Uganda; P353, Long Island.

Typography. Also 'surface-printing' or 'letterpress'—printed from raised type, the actual image being 'in relief', *en épargne* (Fr.), on the printing plate. The die is engraved so that the unwanted parts of the design are cut away. Duplicate impressions are electrotyped or stereotyped from the original die, and these form a printing plate.
Illustrations: P354, GB; P355, Portugal; P356, Russia; P357, Australia; P358, Netherlands; P359, Russia.

Xylography. The art of engraving on wood. Some stamps of Victoria, 1854–59, were true woodblocks, individually engraved to form a plate of 50 impressions. For the 'Registration' and 'Too Late' stamps, separate stereotyped plates for the secondary colours augmented the woodblocks, while in the 'Emblems' issue (1957–60), electrotyped 'plates' were made from woodblock 'dies'.
Illustrations: P360, 361, Victoria, 1854–59.

Proof. Impressions taken during the preparation of the master die or printing plate prior to the manufacture of postage stamps. The various terms (which follow) have been adapted to the specialised procedures of stamp engraving and plate-making, and do not necessarily agree with those of the printing trade. Proofs show the evolution and development of a stamp, and form very interesting additions to a specialised collection.

Engraver's Progress Proofs. Impressions taken by the engraver from a die at frequent intervals, to enable him to check the progress of his work. A series of such proofs, which alas are in limited supply, would show the gradual building-up of the design image.
Illustration: P372, Western Australia—partially completed proof of the One Penny 'Swan'.

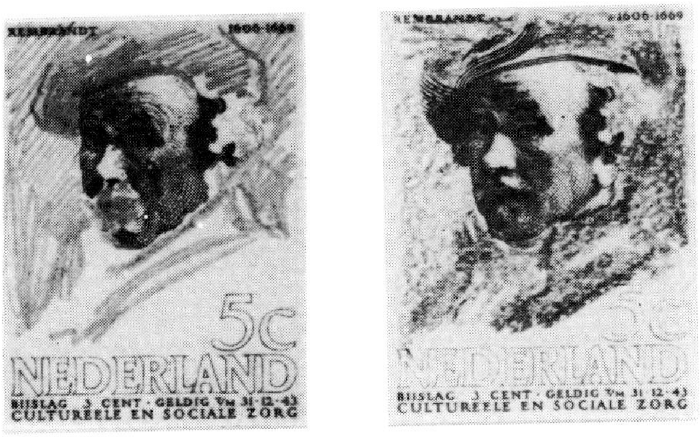

Two engraver's proofs of a Sem Hartz stamp for Netherlands

Die Proofs. The engraver having completed his die, numerous impressions are taken for record purposes and for submission to the stamp-issuing authorities for final approval. Die proofs are normally run off in black, sometimes in other colours (see 'Colour Trials' and 'Colour Proofs'). When the die has been pronounced satisfactory by all concerned, preparations are made for the manufacture of a printing plate or 'stone'.
Illustration: P373, Mauritius die proof.

P372

P373

P374

P375 (PAIR)

P376

P377

P378

P379

P380

P381

P382

P383

P384

P385

P386

P387

P388

P389

P390

P391

P392

P393

P394

P395

P396

P397

P398

P399

P400

P401

P402

Plate Proofs. Now it is the turn of the plate-maker or printer to take impressions from the plate, etched cylinder or 'stone' before printing commences. A careful examination of the proof will reveal whether any 'retouching' or corrections are necessary (see 'Re-engraving'—'Retouching').
Illustrations: P374, South Australia 9d. (line-engraved); P375, Rumania 3b.—pair electrotyped in colour.

Colour Trials. Proofs taken in various selected colours to enable a final choice of colour to be made for a stamp or series of stamps.
Illustrations: P376 to 378, Netherlands 5c. William III, and P379 to 382, 5c. postage dues.

Colour Proofs. Impressions of the approved colours taken prior to the stamps being printed.
Illustrations: P383, 384, France 'Peace and Commerce' and 'Sower' types; P385, Honduras.

Rainbow Proofs. Also 'Trials'. A series of proofs produced by the British authorities between May and December, 1840, and in March and May, 1841, to test various coloured inks, cancellations and paper, the stamps being in the design of the Penny Black. These were distinguished by having the top right (north-east) corners void and by the omission of corner letters.
Illustration: P386, GB 1d. red of May, 1841.

Used Proofs. Trial printings of Lithuania's National Assembly stamps of 1920 were available from post offices for the prepayment of postage. Occasionally proofs of other countries have been used in the post without detection.
Illustrations: P387, Italy 5c. green; P388, 5c. brown proof used in the post.

Propaganda Stamps. Stamps which convey a message of some sort, or designed to further a campaign or cause, either by the inscription, design or both.

Commercial. Various countries have issued stamps featuring their agricultural products, industrial output and trade generally. Really a form of advertising.
Illustrations: P389, Pakistan (Colombo Plan), Cement factory; P390, Upper Volta, 'Voltex' cotton textiles; P391, Sweden, Goteborg, container ships; P392, Poland, Poznan Trade Fair.

Political. Stamps carrying national or political slogans, or having pictorial or symbolic designs relating to current events or their anniversaries.

Illustrations: P393, France, Rural aid; P394, Germany, 'Ein Fuhrer'; P395, Japan, Women's suffrage; P396, Russia, 'More Metal—More Machines!'

Religious. Many stamps are issued with religious subjects, usually to commemorate religious events or holy festivals. Stamps issued by Portugal in 1895 had a prayer in Latin printed on the back.
Illustrations: P397, Bahamas, Christmas; P398, Congo Republic (Brazzaville), Easter; P399, Cayman Islands, Christmas; P400, Brazil, Mothers' Day; P401, Falkland Islands, Consecration of Bishop Stirling; P402, Vatican City, St. Domenico di Guzman.

Tourist. Stamps specially designed and issued to encourage tourism.
Illustrations: P403, Barbados, water-skiing; P404, France, Riom; P405, France, Sedan; P406, Indonesia, musician; P407, Philippine Islands, volcano and train; Thailand, floating market.

Provisional Stamps. Issued for temporary use, usually consisting of overprints and/or surcharges on existing stamps. The usual circumstances necessitating the issue of provisional stamps include a shortage of certain denominations (made good by surcharging the appropriate face value on other values), commemorations or changes in a country's name, sovereignty, government or currency which have occurred at short notice.
Illustrations: P409, Ceylon '3 cents'; P410, Thailand 'Thailandpex 1971' commemorative; P411, Iraq, 'W.M. Day'; P412, Ireland, Easter Rising commemorative; P413, Ecuador, surcharge in words; P414, Colombia, 'provisional'; P415, Salvador, 'provisional'.

Local. When a consignment of low-value stamps failed to arrive in British Central Africa from London in 1898, the Postmaster in Blantyre (Nyasaland Protectorate) authorised the acceptance of cash, in lieu of stamps, for internal letters. Specially-printed adhesive stamps, face value 1d., utilising the current embossed 'cheque' stamp as the main design, were affixed to letters by the authorities to indicate that postage had been paid. They were not issued to the public. Known also as 'cheque stamps'.
Illustration: P416, Nyasaland 'Internal Postage'.

Inter-Provincials. Stamps of member colonies or provinces of a federation or union, used in other colonies or provinces. The term is usually applied to the stamps of the South African colonies of Cape of Good Hope, Natal, Orange Free State and the Transvaal which, from the formation of the Union in 1910, were permitted to be used in other colonies/provinces until 1913. Such usage can only be distinguished by the postmark.
Illustration: P417, Cape stamps used in Harrismith, Orange Free State.

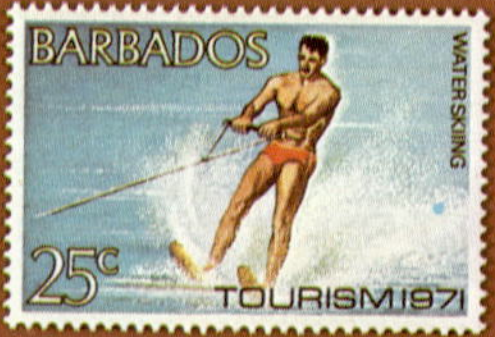

P403

P404

P405

P406

P407

P408

P409

P410

P411

P412

P413

P414

P415

P416

P417

R1

R2

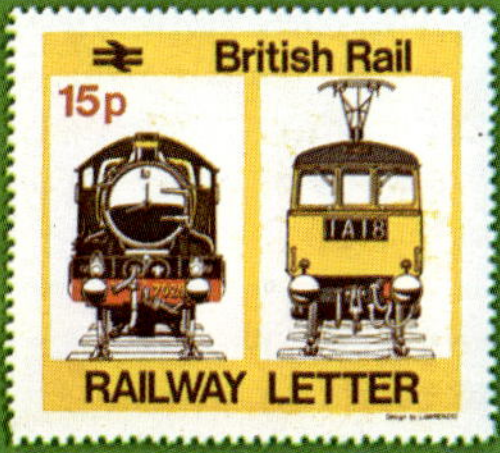

R3

R4

R5

R6

R7

R8

R9

R10

R11

R12

R13

R14

R15

R16

R17

R18

Railway Letter Fee Stamps. Special stamps formerly issued by British railway companies for the conveyance of letters by rail—a kind of 'express' service for which, in addition to a special fee, the normal postal charges were also due.

In May 1957, the Talyllyn Railway in Wales began issuing railway letter stamps, and other local railways followed suit. In October 1971, British Railways, London Midland Region (Birmingham), issued a 15p general railway letter stamp in an attractive design.

Illustrations: R1, North British Railway stamp; R2, Lancashire & Yorkshire Railway 3d. provisional; R3, British Rail 15p railway letter stamp; R4, Caledonian Railway stamp and cancellation.

Recorded Message Stamps. In 1939, Argentina issued stamps for the payment of special fees for postage on gramophone discs bearing recorded messages.

Illustrations: R5 and 6, Argentine Republic recorded message stamps.

Redrawn. A new printing of a stamp whose design differs in some detail from the original, while retaining its principal features. Examples are the Russia 'Arms' types of 1883–88, reissued with 'thunderbolts' added to the posthorns, 1889–94; and the current GB 'Machin' decimal definitives which replaced similar stamps in 'shillings and pence'.

Illustrations: R7, GB 'Penny Lilac' with 14 corner 'pearls'; R8, ditto with 16 'pearls'; R9, 10, Japan 70y 'Noh Mask' original and redrawn types.

Re-engraving. The strengthening of worn parts of the surface of a printing plate by hand-work is termed 're-engraving' or 'recutting', terms also used when an original die is deepened, prior to preparing a new plate.

Illustrations: R11, 13, New Zealand 'Kiwi' and R12, 15, France 'Mont St Michel', original and re-engraved examples.

Retouch. A minor correction effected by hand-engraving on the plate or cylinder. The term is now commonly applied to flaws 'made good' on photogravure-printed stamps.

Illustrations: R14, GB Twopence Blue, retouched frame-line; R16, Switzerland 'Standing Helvetia', weakness of top lines strengthened by cross-hatching.

Registration Stamps. Special stamps, adhesive or impressed on envelopes, denoting the extra fee paid for the additional safeguard of registration. In some cases the number of the letter is inserted on the stamp instead of on the registration label.

Illustrations: R17, Canada registered letter stamp; R18, Colombia 'R' stamp with number.

Canada 'secret mark'—the designer's initials 'GT' (G. Trottier) in the bottom right corner

Re-issues. Stamps issued again after having been withdrawn from use, either from stocks or by fresh printings from the original plates. In some cases, especially in Latin-American countries, postal validity is renewed or confirmed by an overprint such as 'Habilitada' or 'Resellada'. Not to be confused with new printings of current stamps. See 'Reprints'.
Illustrations: R19, Mexico 'Hidalgo' stamp overprinted for use in Guadalajara; R20, Newfoundland 'Codfish'; R21, Bolivia stamp reissued with surcharge.

Remainders. Unsold stamps on hand after an issue has been taken off sale. Such stamps are normally destroyed, but on occasion they are used as the basis of new issues by the means of overprints and/or surcharges. In some cases, remainders have been sold to members of the stamp trade or to private individuals, either in unused state (when they are indistinguishable from the original issue of stamps), or cancelled by some special device such as overprinted bars. 'Postmarked' remainders were usually sold to collectors at much cheaper prices than the original stamps with genuine postmarks indicating postal use. See also 'Cancelled to Order', and 'Reprints'.
Illustrations: R22, Costa Rica; R23, Trinidad; R24, Mexico; R25, Labuan.

Reprints. Stamps, other than re-issues (above), printed from the original plates after the official stamps had ceased to be current, usually to satisfy the demands of collectors. Sometimes the plates were disposed of with the remainders so that the purchaser could print as many more stamps as he wished, as in the case of the infamous Nicholas F. Seebeck who contracted to supply certain Latin-American states with stamps free of charge in the 1890's; in return, he acquired all unsold remainders and the original plates. 'Reprints' is the term also applied by the Crown Agents to new printings of Commonwealth stamps in relation to the normal replenishment of current and permanent definitive issues.
Illustrations: R26, Nicaragua; R27, Victoria fiscal; R28, South Australia 'reprint'; R29, Austria.

Secret Marks. Reference or identification marks in stamp designs, made by the designers, engravers or printers as a kind of 'cachet' of their work, or as distinguishing marks. Examples are Cuba, 10 c. of 1899 and 1905–07—the printers of the second issue, the American Bank Note

R19

R20

R21

R22

R23

R24

R25

R26

R27

R28

R29

S1

S2

S3

S4

S5

S6

S7

S8

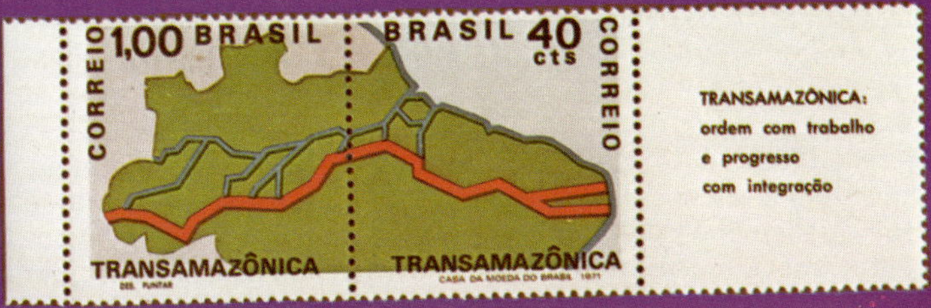

S9

S10

S11

S12

S13

S14

S15

S16

S17

S18

S19

S20

Company, added a small white ball to the extension of the panel containing the word 'CUBA'; and the United States 1 c. Franklin of 1870 and 1873—again the second printers, the Continental Bank Note Company, added a small line on the pearl to the left of the figure '1'.

Some modern engraved issues of Canada have so-called 'secret marks' on them—the year of issue in minute figures, while during the German occupation of the Channel Islands in World War II, 1d. stamps in the normal 'Arms' type were issued with tiny corner letters 'A', representing the defiant slogan *Ad Avernum Adolf Atrox* ('To Hell with you, atrocious Adolf'). Later, a similar device castigating both Hitler and Mussolini appeared on the ½d. stamp.

So-called 'date-cuts' were used by Somerset House in printing the GB Edward VII stamps, taking the form of a double cut in the marginal rule (or 'Jubilee line') under the 11th or penultimate stamp of the bottom row in the sheet, representing the year of printing, i.e. 1911, or under the 12th or last stamp—1912. Prior to this, the original printers, De La Rue, had used the same method for marking and identifying the different plates.

Illustrations: S1, Cuba, ball added; S2, GB Edward VII 1½d. with date-cut (1912); S3, US 1 c., line on pearl.

Serial Numbers. The series numbering of sheets and miniature sheets of stamps has been used by many countries as a means of controlling and checking numbers printed. These usually appear in the sheet margins, though in the case of Spanish issues, serial sheet numbers may be found imprinted on the backs of individual stamps. Modern security printers have sophisticated machines for counting and numbering sheets of stamps as they are printed.

Illustrations: S4, GB 3p 'Machin' with serial and cylinder numbers; S5, S. Rhodesia; S6, Israel.

Se-tenant. A French term meaning 'joined together', used to describe adjoining stamps which differ from each other in value, design, or in some other respect such as one overprinted or surcharged, and the other not. It has become common practice to include two or more different designs—arranged horizontally side-by-side, or vertically *se-tenant*—in the one sheet of stamps (see 'Sheet Composite'). In some cases, pairs or larger combinations of stamps form a composite design, these being arranged *se-tenant* within the sheet. Stamp booklets often contain *se-tenant* stamps and/or labels (see 'Sheet-Composite'). *Tête-bêche* varieties, adjoining stamps inverted in relation to each other, have a *se-tenant* arrangement.

Illustrations: S7, Belgium, one stamp surcharged; S8, Gabon, narrow and wide settings of surcharge; S9, Brazil, pair with different face values and composite design plus se-tenant label; S10, Rumania, se-tenant designs.

Setting. Type for printing is composed or 'set' by the compositor, hence a setting is a particular arrangement or grouping of movable types or clichés forming a plate or single unit. The term is used principally in connexion with overprinted and/or surcharged stamps where there may be one setting, i.e. plate, for a sheet of stamps, or perhaps four or six matrices or stereotyped plates to make up the sheet. In the latter event the actual formation of the whole plate may be deduced by the study of individual clichés—distinctive flaws such as broken letters or other irregularities would be recurring at fixed intervals on the plate. In the same way, second and third settings etc. may be identified.
Illustrations: S11, 12, Rhodesia 'Half Penny' settings, one with hyphen and full stop; S13, 14, Turks & Caicos Islands, different settings of 'War Tax'.

Shade. A variety or degree of colour—in philately the term implies a variation, gradation or difference in the tonal depth. A 'shade' ceases to be such when the variation is sufficiently marked to alter the basic colour of the stamp. For example a green stamp tending to blue-green and turquoise would, if the progression continued, become greenish blue, i.e. basically blue.

Shades usually occur in new printings of definitive stamps, when the printers are unable to match exactly the printing inks used in the original or preceding issue, or when climatic changes take place. Marked shades, which may be linked to specific printings of stamps and the relative sheet cylinder or plate numbers, are recorded in *Gibbons Catalogues* (except *Stamps of the World*), but not where there is a whole range of intermediate shades.
Illustrations: Shades of, S15, 16, Sweden 5 öre; S17, 18, Canada 1 cent; S19, 20, USA 2 cents.

Sheet of Stamps. Stamps are printed on sheets of paper trimmed to convenient size or, if printed 'on the web', i.e. on continuous reels, subsequently guillotined to 'sheet' size. The size of a sheet and the number of stamps contained within it may vary from the very small, e.g. Czechoslovakia, 4 stamps (*not* a 'miniature sheet'), to the current GB 'Machin' low-value definitives in sheets of 200.

Generally, 'printer's sheets' contain two or four panes which are cut into separate 'post office' sheets for easy handling. The number of stamps in a 'post office' sheet is usually related to a country's currency, and sheets of 60, 120 or 240 stamps were commonly used in GB and Commonwealth countries, whose monetary systems were based on sterling pounds, shillings and pence, i.e. 240 pence to the pound. Most countries now have decimal currencies with sheets of 50, 100 or 200 stamps. Smaller sheets of 30 subjects are coming into use in some Commonwealth countries. Modern Swedish stamps are not issued in sheets, but in rolls for automatic vending machines, or in booklets. See also 'Imprint', 'Margin', 'Marginal Guide Marks' and 'Marginal Inscriptions'.

S21

S22

S23

S24

S25

S26

S27

S28

Composite Sheet. A sheet of stamps made up of different values, types or designs, or a normal sheet overprinted or surcharged in a similar manner, enabling a complete unit or set of stamps to be obtained from a single sheet. In modern practice, such stamps are usually arranged in joined (*se-tenants*) pairs, blocks of four or larger combinations. Sheets specially printed for cutting up and binding into booklets may have a composite arrangement. Also see 'Panes'.
Illustrations: S21, Jaipur, mixed values; S22, Germany, part of sheet intended for booklets; S23, USA 'Wildlife'; S24, St. Lucia 'Old and New'.

Miniature Sheet. A small sheet containing a single stamp, pair, block or set of stamps, with wide, inscribed and/or decorative margins, issued as a commemorative souvenir for collectors. Some, but not all, have postal validity in sheet form.
Illustrations: S25, USA 'Farley' min. sheet of 1936; S26, Bolivia 'Flora'.

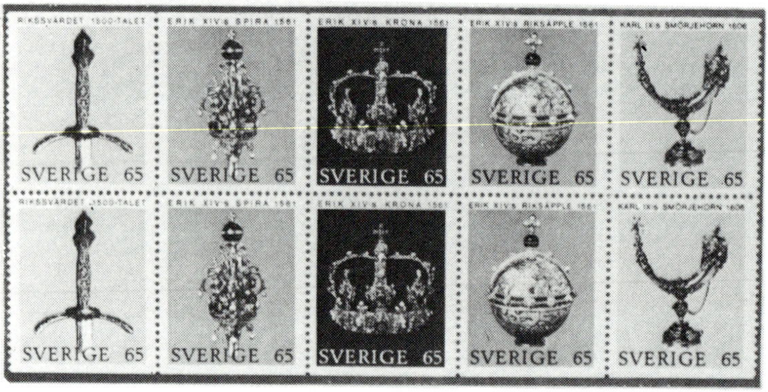

Regalia from the Royal Treasury —
a Swedish booklet pane with se-tenant pairs

Pane. The sub-section or part of a sheet of stamps, usually separated by 'gutter' margins; also a leaf of 2, 3, 4 or 6 or more stamps in a booklet.
Illustrations: S27, GB 'Machin' booklet pane with se-tenant stamps: S28 New Zealand booklet pane.

Shrinkage. Paper shrinkage, resulting from the alternate dampening and drying of sheets of line-engraved stamps in the printing process, has sometimes caused minute variations in the actual size of stamps, or their designs. Examples may be found in the stamps of Chile, Columbus, 1905–09, and Gibraltar, KGV, 1931–33.

Decorative spandrel in the GB Edward VII 1d. design

Sinking Fund Stamps. For some years (1927–31) the French postal authorities made a bi-annual issue of stamps specially inscribed or overprinted 'Caisse d' Amortissement', or 'CA'. These stamps were sold for postage in the usual way, but an extra premium was charged over and above the normal postal rates, the premium being transferred to a fund for the reduction of the national debt.
Illustrations: S29, 'Sower' type of 1928; S30, Pictorial type (1928); S31, 'Pasteur' type of 1928.

Spandrel. The space or decorative portion of a stamp design between the outer rectangular border or frame and the central circle, oval or similar form (other than rectangular) enclosing the main part of the design.
Illustrations: S32, India; S33, Monaco; S34, GB QV 5s.; and S35, St. Kitts-Nevis.

Special Fee Stamps. Issued for various special services. Danish stamps overprinted or inscribed 'Gebyr' or 'Gebyrmaerke' were used to indicate that certain fees had been paid, including the late registration of letters.
Illustrations: S36, 'Gebyr' overprint (1923); S37, 'Gebyrmaerke' inscription (1926–30).

Late Fee Stamps. Used for the prepayment of additional postal fees to enable a letter to catch a certain mail after the normal collection has been effected. 'Retardo' on the stamps of Latin-American countries.
Illustrations: S38, Colombia; S39, Panama.

Marine Insurance Stamps. Issued in Holland in 1921 to prepay the fee for the inclusion of letters in a patent safe, unsinkable in the event of shipwreck and comparatively indestructible in the case of fire aboard the vessel.
Illustration: S40, Netherlands 15c. 'Druvende Brandkast'.

S29
S30
S31
S32
S33
S34
S35
S36
S37
S38
S39
S40
S41
S42
S43
S44
S45
S46

S47

S48

S49

S50

S51

S52

S53

S54

S55

S56

S57

S58

S59

S60

S61

Porte de Mar. Stamps so inscribed were issued by Mexico in 1875 and used, in conjunction with the normal postage stamps, to indicate the fees due to be paid to the owners of the British and French mail-boats, on letters transported by them.
Illustration: S41, Mexico 10c. 'Porte de Mar'.

Specimen. Samples of new stamps, distributed to the various countries of the world through the offices of the UPU for purposes of identification and record, are inscribed, overprinted or punch-perforated with the word 'Specimen' or its foreign equivalent. Specimen stamps are often available to collectors—some early issues are highly prized—and certain issuing authorities distribute 'samples' to the philatelic press. 'Specimen' is also synonymous with the word 'stamp', meaning 'example'—'a good specimen' or a good example.
Illustrations; S42, GB QV ½d. overprinted; S43, Malaya FMS 'Tiger' punch-perforated; S44, Spain 'Muestra' opt; S45, Cyprus optd.; S46, Germany (West Berlin) 'Muster' opt.

Speculative Issues. Stamps issued (1) almost exclusively for the 'benefit' of collectors, usually commemoratives with little or no postal requirements, or (2) deliberately in reduced quantities to encourage speculation and high prices with a quick profit for the sponsors. The stamp issues of certain Central and South American States, organised by N. F. Seebeck, were highly speculative. (See 'Reprints'.)

In modern times, speculation has taken the trend of purchasing large quantities (or 'portfolios') of commemorative stamps to be 'held' for future appreciation, a procedure which not only ultimately disrupts the stamp market and the value of the stamps, but also invariably involves the impatient speculator in a loss.
Illustrations: 'Seebecks' of, S47, Honduras; S48, Salvador; S49, Nicaragua.

Split Stamps. Parts of stamps which (1) have been specially designed to be subdivisible, as the 'quarters' of the 19th-century issues of Brunswick and Mecklenburg-Schwerin, or (2) have been split—usually bisected—for use in emergencies such as shortage of supplies, equivalent to a proportion of the original 'whole' face value or as amended by an appropriate surcharge. In the used state, split stamps are best collected on the original envelope or 'piece', showing the part-stamp 'tied' by the postmark.

Bisect. Half of a stamp which has been cut or perforated in two to furnish an authorised denomination of half the original face value, or otherwise surcharged. Bisects are commonly found with horizontal or diagonal cuts, occasionally with vertical divisions. They were mostly cut with knife or scissors, but those issued in Portuguese India, Lourenzo Marques and Argentina were specially surcharged

and perforated. The parcel-post stamps of Italy and San Marino are sold in divisible two-part units, one of which forms the receipt.
Illustrations: S50, British Honduras; S51, Uruguay; S52, Lourenzo Marques; S53, Portuguese India; S54, Argentina; S55, Belgium.

Quarter. A fourth part of a divisible stamp as issued by certain German states (see above). Brunswick's '4/4' stamps, issued in 1857, had a face value of 1 gutegroschen (or 12 pf.)—the $\frac{1}{4}$ ggr. sections could be separately used for the lowest postal rate i.e. local printed matter.
Illustrations: S56, Brunswick 4/4 ggr.; S57, Brunswick, composite use of a pair and single $\frac{1}{4}$ ggr. stamps.

Trimmed. In order to provide a provisional postage stamp of 6 annas face value in 1886, the Indian authorities converted some fiscal stamps of that value by trimming the upper and lower portions, and overprinting the remainder with the word 'Postage'. A similar procedure was adopted in the Portuguese Colony of Macao in 1887, and in 1903, French Indian Settlements' fiscal stamps were bisected, the upper halves being overprinted and surcharged. In 1892, postage stamps of Ecuador, which had been overprinted for official and telegraph purposes, were re-converted for ordinary postage by the removal of the top portions of the stamps bearing the 'Official' and 'Telegraph' overprints.
Illustrations: S58, India, converted fiscal; S59, Ecuador overprinted official, and S60, with opt. trimmed; S61, Macao surcharged fiscal.

Stamp Currency. Unused postage stamps authorised for use as 'coins' during shortages, notably in the American Civil War, and in Russia, 1915–18. The latter were printed on card and inscribed on the back that the stamps had circulation on a par with subsidiary silver coins (or copper money). Stamps used as money in Belgium and France during the 1914–18 War encased and known as counters or 'jetons'.
Illustrations: S62, 63, Russia 1917 1k and 3k; S64, Ukraine 1918 10 shagiv.

Stamp Duty. An inscription common to fiscal stamps, also found on the early postage stamps of the Australian States and New Zealand etc., all (with the exception of Victoria from 1884) being classified as 'postal fiscals'. The Victoria Government's Postage Act of 1883, decreed the stamps of the three existing types—postage, duty and fee—to be interchangeable, and that there should be one multi-purpose stamp series in use from the beginning of 1885. These continued to be inscribed 'Stamp Duty' up to and including the issues of 1896–99.
Illustrations: S65, Victoria 1885; S66, Victoria 1890; Victoria 1887–96; S68, New Zealand 1882; S69 Tasmania 1880.

S62

S63

S64

S65

S66

S68

S67

S69

S70

S71

S72

S75

S73

S74

S76

S77

S78

S79

S80

S81

S82

S83

S84

S85

S86

S87

S88

S89

S90

S91

S92

S93

S94

Stamped Paper. A term denoting paper bearing an impressed fiscal stamp, not applicable to postal stationery.
Illustration: S70, 'Bill or note. Threepence'.

Straight Edge. The imperforate side(s) of a normally-perforated stamp, commonly found among American and Canadian stamps due to the division of gutter margins between sheets (or panes) by guillotine. Stamps from booklets and coils (or rolls) are also found with straight edges which, however, are generally termed 'imperforate at side' etc.
Illustrations: S71, Sweden booklet stamps; S72, 73, Australian coils; S74, 76, US 1c. Franklin; S75, US 6c. Airmail (booklet).

Strip. Three or more stamps joined in a single row, horizontal or vertical.
Illustration: S77, China, strip of 3 also arranged se-tenant and forming a composite design.

Sulphuretted. Or 'oxidised'. Descriptive of stamps in certain colours —red, orange, yellow etc.—which have turned to deep brown or black due to chemical action on the printing ink.
Illustrations: S78, Newfoundland; S79, GB 'Penny Red'; S80, China; S81, Canada.

Surcharge. An overprint which alters or establishes a stamp's face value.
Illustrations: S82, Samoa; S83, Australia; S84, Chile; S85, Transvaal; S86, British Levant; S87, Chile; S88, 89, Cook Islands; S90, New Zealand.

Manuscript. A provisional surcharge applied by pen and ink.
Illustration: S91, Trinidad 1d. of 1882, surcharged by hand.

Typewritten. Tonga issued typewritten, surcharged stamps in 1896.
Illustration: S92, Tonga $\frac{1}{2}$d. on 7$\frac{1}{2}$d. on 2d.

'Vale' Surcharge on Back. In 1911, certain railway stamps of Nicaragua, which had been surcharged for fiscal use, were further surcharged on the back for postage.
Illustration: S93, Nicaragua 5c. provisional.

Syllabic Characters. Small characters representing the plate-numbers found on Japanese stamps and postal stationery of 1874–75.
Illustration: S94, Japan $\frac{1}{2}$ sen of 1874 showing plate no. 1 in Katakana (syllabic alphabet).

Israel stamp for the inauguration of the Knesset (Parliament) Building—with tab

Tab. An appendage to a stamp in the form of an attached coupon, label or 'tag'. The Dominical labels (page 53) are tabs of a kind, but the best-known examples are those consistently found in the sheet margins (usually at the foot) of Israel stamps. These invariably have pictorial and/or descriptive motifs related to the stamp designs, the stamps being collected with the tabs attached.
Illustration: T1, Israel tab.

Telegraph Stamps. Adhesive or imprinted stamps intended solely for the prepayment of telegraph communications and usually attached to, or forming part of, the message form. Telegraph stamps are appropriately described—e.g., 'Telegrafo(s)' in Spanish-speaking countries —and are a popular sideline with collectors. Also known postally used, but difficult to identify as such unless preserved on the original cover. Conversely, ordinary postage stamps have been used for telegraphic purposes and here again such usage is difficult to establish with loose stamps.
Illustrations: T2, GB QV 1d.; T3, Cuba 10c.; T4, Chile 20c.; T5, Spanish Tangier 1p.

Military Telegraphs. Stamps overprinted or inscribed for use by H.M. Forces while on active service abroad, between 1884 and 1901.
Illustrations: T6, 7, GB QV 2d. and $\frac{1}{2}$d. (*overprinted*) *'Army Telegraphs'.*

Tête-bêche. A term of French origin applied particularly to a joined pair of stamps in which one is upside-down in relation to the other.
Illustrations: T8, Belgium; T9, West Germany; T10, Switzerland; T11, Hungary (*also imperf.–between*)*; T12, Philippine Islands* (*two different, surcharged designs*).

T1

T2

T3

T4

T5

T6

T7

T8

T9

T10

T11

T12

T13

T14

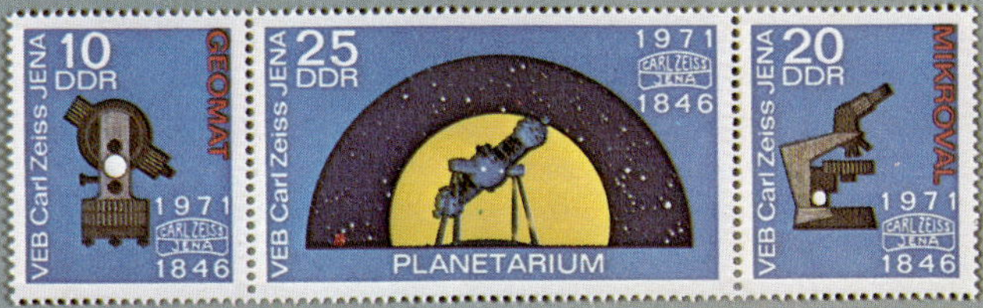

T15

T16

T17

U1

U2

U3

U4

U5

U6

U7

U8

U9

U10

U11

U12

U13

Thematic Collecting. Or 'Thematics'. The popular method of collecting stamps with a specific pictorial subject or theme, such as Birds, Flowers, Ships, Sport and numerous others. Virtually every modern stamp can be related to one or other theme, which may also be extended to embrace pictorial postmarks. Known in the United States as 'Topical' collecting.
Illustration: T13, 'Paintings'—Rumania, 'Venus and Amor' (*Il Vecchio*).

Tied. Adhesive stamps 'married' to the original envelope, postcard or wrapper, by the postmark which extends beyond the confines of the stamp on to the postal matter, confirming the genuine use of the original item. The term 'tied' is also applied to stamps 'on piece', and is particularly desirable in the case of bisected stamps used in the post.
Illustration: T14, Kuwait tied stamp and postmark.

Toughra. A paraph, signature or flourish of the Sultan appearing on early Turkish stamps as a mark of authenticity.
Illustrations: T16, 17, Turkish stamps of 1901 and 1916.

Triptych. A philatelic term 'borrowed' from the art world and having the same meaning—'a set of three panels or tablets, etc., hinged together,' applied to three joined stamps of different, though related, designs.
Illustration: T15, East Germany, 1971 Carl Zeiss commemoratives.

U.P.U. The well-known initials of the Universal Postal Union, Berne, which was founded in 1874 and which unites all the countries of the world with organised postal services in an established policy of international co-operation. The abbreviation 'U.P.U.' may be found on many of the earlier stamps of the Central and South American Republics who are members of the Union.
Illustrations: U1, Costa Rica (*surcharge*)*; U2, Honduras.*

Ungummed stamps. The majority of stamps are provided with gum or mucilage on the back in order that they may be affixed to correspondence and so perform their postal function. Even the world's first stamps, the Penny Black and Twopence Blue, were coated on the backs with 'cement' which the user was admonished 'not to remove' by an instruction in the sheet margin. Unused stamps may be ungummed for one or two main reasons, (1) issued thus in a hot, moist climate, notably in the Far East, to prevent sheets of stamps sticking together, or (2) due to mishap, e.g. having been stuck down and subsequently washed. In the latter category, unused stamps without gum are not favoured by collectors. The catalogue lists provide notes on stamps officially issued without gum.
Illustrations: U3, Japan; U4, Surinam; U5, Brazil (*adhesive paper with no apparent gum*)*; U8, China; U9, North Vietnam; U10, North Korea.*

Unissued Stamps. Those which have been officially prepared, but for some reason—possibly a serious defect or error in design, have not been issued for postal use. Usually noted in the catalogue as 'Prepared for use but not issued.' Some Sudanese 'Self-Government' stamps of 1954 (wrongly inscribed '1953') fell into this category, and were released in error at the Sudan Agency in London. They had no postal validity, however.
Illustrations: U6, Mauritius; U7, Haiti.

Unofficial Stamps. Stamps issued as 'locals' (q.v.) or by private individuals or organisations without the authority or licence of the appropriate postal administration.
Illustrations: U11, Lundy Island '½ puffin'; U12, Provincial Airways 3d.; U13, South Africa 1d. (1901).

Semi-official. Stamps issued by mail-transport organisations which have received partial or tacit recognition by the postal authorities. Examples are the SCADTA air stamps of Colombia, the Great Western Railway Company air stamps of 1933 for the Rail-Air Service, and the various Canadian air stamps for which the Post Office acted as agents only.
Illustrations: U14, Brazil 'Condor'; U15, Canada 'Laurentide Air Service'; U16, Colombia 'SCADTA'.

Unused. The term signifying that a stamp has not been used in the post and is consequently not postmarked or otherwise defaced, though it may be partially or wholly without gum, or bear traces of old hinges on the back. Also see under 'Gum'.
Illustrations: Early issues likely to have hinge-marks—U17, Newfoundland 1870; U19, Argentine Republic 1892–95.

Mint. A stamp in its original state of issue, unused and with full gum (if so issued). In 'mint condition', i.e. as issued by the post office. The insistence by some collectors for 'unmounted mint' stamps (which are kept in stock books and never hinged or mounted in albums) has become a kind of fetish. Carried to extremes it would virtually be impossible to complete even a representative collection of the older stamps in the 'unmounted mint' state.

Details of the different types of gum used in the production of British and Commonwealth stamps may be found in the preliminaries to the appropriate *Gibbons Catalogue.*
Illustrations: U18, GB pair of PUC ½d; U20–22, Mint definitive (Perak, Malaysia), airmail (Samoa) and commemorative (United Nations) stamps.

U14

U15

U16

U17

U18

U19

U20

U21

U22

U23

U24

U25

U26

U27

U28

U29

U30

U31

U32

U33

U34

V1

V2

V3

V4

V5

V6

Used. A stamp which has had postal or fiscal use and has been accordingly postmarked or cancelled. 'Fine used' implies that the postmark is light but sharp and clear, and that a sufficient proportion of it appears on the stamp to facilitate identification (and, preferably, the date of use), although this is not an essential qualification.
Illustrations: U23–25, Set of 3 Singapore stamps with light cancellations; U26 'Man on Moon' stamp with postmark clear of main design.

Used Abroad. The stamps of one country used and postmarked in another country. For many years British stamps were used in British possessions and other places abroad, prior to the issue of definitive stamps in those places. Similarly, the stamps of other countries, notably France and Spain, have been 'used abroad'. Such usage can only be confirmed by the postmark.
Illustration: U27, GB stamp used in Malta.

Used Fiscally. Or 'fiscally used'—postage or 'postage and revenue' stamps used for the payment of revenue charges, such as receipts, stamp duty on documents and bills etc., usually distinguished by the style, colour or wording of the cancellation.
Illustrations: U28, Iceland; U29, India; U30, GB 'Glasgow Corporation'; U31, Gold Coast 'Bank of British West Africa'.

Used on Cover or Entire. A stamp (or stamps) postmarked and preserved on the original envelope, wrapper or postcard etc. Desirable in the case of early stamps with interesting postmarks, airmail 'flown' covers and other instances in which the *entire* letter is of value.
Illustration: U32, GB Penny Red on entire.

Used on Piece. Stamp retained on a portion of the original cover to preserve the entire postmark.
Illustrations: U33, US oval cancellation; U34, Australian stamp and slogan cancellation.

Value Converted. When Mexican paper currency depreciated in value in 1916–18, various stamps were overprinted with a device signifying that the face value was raised to par with the new 'Infalsificable' paper money.
Illustrations: V1, 2, Mexico 'value converted' stamps.

Value Inserted. Stamps printed without specific values, these being inserted prior to issue.
Illustration: V3, Barbacoas (Colombia) type-set provisional of 1901–3 with value and date inserted in manuscript.

Value Typewritten. Albania issued hand-stamped provisionals in 1913 with the face values typewritten in violet.
Illustrations: V4–6, Albania 1913, 10 and 20 para, 2 grosh.

A striking variety—
'missing Queen's head'

Variety. A stamp differing in some visible detail of its manufacture from the normal issue, caused by a fault in the process of printing. *Errors* of colour, design, perforation, etc. are also sometimes loosely termed 'varieties', but with varieties we are primarily concerned with machine faults on specific stamps, which range from the comparatively insignificant or minor flaw (having no exceptional value) to the most striking and/or rare fault (which may be priced at several pounds, even hundreds of pounds, e.g. for a missing Queen's head, GB S.G. 632a and 633a).

Albino. Lacking in colour. A stamp thus printed showing as a colourless impression due to a fortuitous omission of ink or by the interpolation of paper on the printing cylinder or plate. Embossed stamps or postal stationery items were especially prone to albino impressions, which also occur with overprints and surcharges.
Illustrations: V7, US 2c. embossed envelope, normal and V8, albino impression; V9, V10, Peru 1868 1d. 'Porte Franco' green, litho and embossed, normal and albino.

Broken Letters. Caused by damage to, or deterioration of the printing plate, cylinder or type.
Illustrations: V11, Denmark, malformed 'S', V12, Montenegro, broken and dropped 'I'; V13, G.B. 1½d., 'F' for 'E' in 'PENCE'; V14, Newfoundland, broken 'U' in 'BEAUMONT'.

Capped Numerals. Flaws resembling caps surmounting the figures '2' of the United States 2c. 'Washington' definitive of 1890–93.
Illustration: V17, US 2c. with capped '2'.

Clipped Transfer & Cut Edge. Over-close trimming of the paper transfers formerly laid down on the stone in lithography, resulting in the variety known as 'clipped transfer', shown on the stamp as 'cut close' or with parts of the border or frame missing. Similarly, in typography or surface-printing, a part of a cliché carelessly trimmed away, resulting in a 'cut edge' stamp.
Illustrations: V20, Argentine Republic 1858 15c. showing clipped transfer variety.

V7 V8 V9 V10 V11 V12 V13 V14 V15 V16 V17 V18 V19 V20 V21 V22 V23 V24 V25 V26

V27

V28

V29

V30

V31

V32

V33

V34

V35

V36

V37

V38

V39

Colour Changeling. A stamp which has changed colour due to chemical or climatic influences. Some striking colour changelings are caused by consistent exposure to sunlight, and when deliberately contrived the stamp is termed a 'fake'.
Illustrations: V15, 16, GB ½d. of 1880—normal green and changeling blue; V18, 19, Brazil 100 r. of 1882—normal olive-green and changeling orange-brown.

Cracked Plate. Fairly common in the early days of stamp printing, cracks in plates were caused either by undue pressure or by deterioration through 'wear and tear', evident on the printed stamps by coloured or 'clear' (white) lines corresponding to the cracks.
Illustrations: V21, 22, Mexico 1856, and Costa Rica 1863, printed from cracked plates.

Creased Transfer. In lithographic printing—a paper transfer which has been creased or distorted when laid down on the stone, showing on the printed stamp as a compression or defect.
Illustration: V23, Oldenburg 1859 ⅓g.

Découpage. From the French. A means of adjusting the pressure of the printing plate by 'cut-outs' or built-up overlays to obtain lighter or deeper impressions as required. Misalignment resulted in exaggerated light or dark patches.
Illustrations: Greece 1872, V24, Découpage too low; V25, too much to right.

Double Letters. On the early British stamps, the check letters in the corners were punched on the printing-plate by hand, and sometimes the artisan, being dissatisfied with the letter, would erase it and punch it again. In some cases, traces of the first attempt remained and, not coinciding with the final letter, caused the effect of a double impression.
Illustration: V26, GB Penny Red, alphabet letter 'P' doubled.

Dropped Letters. During the printing of type-set stamps or overprints and surcharges, the type may work loose in the forme, and letters and figures may get out of alignment or drop out altogether.
Illustrations: V27, Hungary (Szeged) 1919 Missing 'z' in 'Szeged', and V28, '1' in '1919'; V29, Zanzibar 1895, Dropped 'z' in opt.; V30, Poland 1918, Dropped 'a' in 'Poczta'.

Dry Print. A stamp having a weak or 'thin' appearance, due to any one of several causes—printing ink insufficiently fluid; paper too dry; wiping of cylinder or plate too severe.
Illustration: V31, Dominica 1908.

Hand-painted. Colour applied to a stamp by hand after printing. Almost unheard of these days, but in more leisurely times it was a fairly common practice—an example is the German 5 m. stamp of 1900 on which, in some instances, the red central design did not 'register' accurately with the black frame. The resulting gap was touched up in red, and the overlap in white.
Illustration: V32, Germany 1900 5 m.

More elaborate painting is found on labels issued on Columbia in early years in which the colours of the flag design were applied by hand. These labels were attached to registered packets containing cash, and were handed back to the postman by the recipient after delivery.
Illustration: V33, Columbia 'certification' label.

Inking Faults. Splashes, smudges and blobs due to over-inking, faulty wiping or 'muck' on the plate or cylinder.
Illustrations: V34, Ceylon; V35, South Africa; V36 Switzerland.

Inserted by Hand. A minor type of hand-painting in which missing letters, accents etc., usually in type-set overprints, have been touched in on the stamp.
Illustration: V37, Ireland 1922, Accent inserted by hand.

Ivory Head. The name given to GB Victorian stamps, notably the 1d. and 2d. issues of 1841, of the 'blued' variety, which show the Queen's head in white on the back—the 'blueing' was caused by the addition of prussiate of potash to the printing-ink to render it fugitive. It was most intense where the ink was thickest on the front of the stamp, hence the head (being lightly inked) showed the least blueing or, in the so-called 'ivory heads', virtually none at all.
Illustrations: V38, 39, GB 1d. red and 2d. blue ivory heads.

Misplaced. Among the many contingencies that can, and do, occur in stamp printing are the misplacements, or shifts 'out of register', of parts of the design or its colours, overprints, perforations and watermarks.

The corner (alphabet) letters on early GB stamps, individually punched by hand, were often misplaced, while in modern recess printing, where separate parts of a stamp design—usually vignette (or central design) and frame—require two or more plates and a corresponding number of insertions in the press, shifts of one or other element, due to inaccurate registration, were fairly commonplace.

Colour shifts in modern photogravure printing processes are also 'run-of-the-mill', and occur with such frequency and in such variety that they are not given catalogue recognition.

V40 V41 V42 V43

V44 V45 V46

V47

V48 V49

V50 V51

V52 V53 V54

V55

V56

V57

V58

V59

V60

V61

V62

V63

V64

V65

Illustrations: V40, GB Penny Red; V41, British East Africa with single Crown CA watermark; V42, Martinique surcharge; V43, United States 8 c. booklet stamp 'off centre'; V44, Bulgaria, downward shift of vignette; V45, Dominican Republic, sideways shift of vignette; V46, Russia, misplaced arms and figure of value; V47, Salvador, 'Garl' for 'Gral' in overprint; V48, Botswana, three versions of 2½ c. 'National Assembly Building' flag showing normal (centre) *and shifts of deep blue band; V49, Tonga, close '3d—XX' surcharge variety.*

Mixed Printer s Type. Mixed style of type used accidentally or out of necessity (due to an inadequate supply of one style or size of type).
Illustrations: V50, Nicaragua, 'surcharged on back'; V51, Guatemala, small 's' in 'CENTAVOS'; V52, New Zealand, large 'F' in 'OFFICIAL', and V53, broken 'E' used for first 'F'.

Palimpsest. 'A manuscript or parchment in which old writing has been rubbed out to make room for new'. The philatelic application of the term is seen on a Mexican stamp where traces of the figure '10' are visible just below the upper right-hand value tablet.
Illustration: V54, Mexico 1874 25 c.

Part Impressions. Stamps which have received only a partial impression from the printing plate or cylinder, due to a production fault. See also 'Printer's Waste'.
Illustration: V55, Brazil, part of red colour missing.

Part Perforated. Stamps inadvertently issued partially perforated (or partially imperforate) due to technical faults.
Illustrations: V56, 57, Greece; V58, Mexico.

Printing Flaws. Some examples of the most common flaws and corrections occurring in the various printing processes.
Illustrations: Photogravure—V59, South West Africa, white patch above '3'; V60, S. Rhodesia, retouched patch in pioneer's hat; V61, GB 8d. 'Wilding', extra pearl in earring; V62, Mauritius, dot between 'U' and 'S' of 'MAURITIUS'. Recess—V63, Barbados, part of shading missing in top border at right. Lithography—V64, British Indian Ocean Territory, 'ring' flaw. Typography—V65, GB KGV, 'No Cross on Crown'.

Re-entry on the Canada 3d. 'Beaver' note the doubling of the '3'

Re-entry. A term used in philately to indicate a double impression, usually of a small portion of the design, that may be found on certain stamps printed by the line-engraved process. The duplication is the result of a second application of the transfer roller upon the printing plate, in a position which is not identical with that of the original entry, and causing signs of both entries to appear on the printed stamp. If the second entry is made during the preparation of the plate, the technical terms used are 'shift'—a failure of the transfer roller to match the original rolling-in on the reverse or return 'run', or 'fresh entry'—a design entered a second time over a faulty and incompletely-erased entry.

Strictly, the term 're-entry' should be applied to instances of re-entering an engraved plate at some stage *after* it has been used for printing, necessitated by wear or damage. If the new entry exactly matches the lines of the original impression, the (subsequently) printed stamp will show evidence of the deeper entry. Failure to coincide with the original entry will result in duplication, at least in part, of the design—known as a 'non-coincident' re-entry.

Illustration: V66, Peru—pair of 1s. (1886) showing whole stamp double (left), and normal (right).

The term 'double strike' is used in the case of stamps printed by typography, where the duplication is produced by a faulty impression of the die on the mould from which the unit is electrotyped or stereotyped.

Similarly, 'double transfer' denotes the same effect in the lithographic process, caused by a misplaced or misshapen transfer on the litho 'stone'.

Illustrations: V67, Victoria 1d. with 'ONE' double: (typo) V68, Seychelles KGV 50 c. with entire head plate double (typo); V69, Peru 1d. of 1858 with north-east quarter doubled (litho) and V70, normal.

V66

V67

V68

V69

V70

V71

V72

V73

V74

V75

V76

V77

V78

V79

V80

V81

V82

V83 V84 V85

W1 W2 W3

W4 W5 W6 W7

W8 W9 W10 W11 W12

W13 W14 W15

Reversed Print. Stamps printed in reverse, by accident or design, also known as 'mirror prints' because of their visual effect. The 10 and 30 silbergroschen stamps issued by Prussia in 1866 were deliberately printed in reverse on the back of transparent paper, allowing the design to show through the front. See 'Resinised Paper'. In lithography, a reversed transfer, and in photogravure, a reversed negative, would result in a mirror print.

Illustrations: V71, Syria, part of imprint, 'Vaugirard', reversed (photogravure); V72, Peru, reversed litho.

Set-off. A form of reversed print, caused by laying a sheet of stamps on another printed sheet which has been insufficiently dried, resulting in a 'transfer' of the design images to the gummed underside of the upper sheet, in reverse. 'Set-off' is preferable to 'offset' which is a lithographic term.

A similar variety can occur in printing if a sheet of paper fails to be taken up by the rollers, and a 'wild' impression on the underlay or impression cylinder is transferred to the back of the next sheet, known as a 'blanket print'.

Illustrations: V73, Spain; V74, Rhodesia (pair); V75, Colombia.

Setting Error. A cliché laid-down sideways or upside-down in relation to the others on a printing plate or lithographic stone.

Illustration: V76, Rumania (Moldo-Wllachia) 1864, pair of 6 p. with stamp turned sideways.

Smudged (or Slurred) Print. Indistinct blur or doubling of a stamp design caused by 'paper-slip' at the point of contact with the printing cylinder or plate. Not a true 'double print'.

Illustrations: V77, Mexico; V78, US official, unsufficiently wiped; V79, Newfoundland; V80, Bolivia.

Watermark Error. Stamps may be found with part or all of the watermark missing due to a broken or missing 'bit'—the shaped metal design of the watermark impressed in the paper pulp during manufacture. British Commonwealth stamps are known with a St Edward's Crown in place of the normal Tudor Crown, due to an error in replacing a faulty or missing bit. Similarly, two crowns of entirely different shape are found in certain sheets of the Large Crown watermarked paper used in Great Britain between 1854 and 1864. A common error is the watermark inverted (in relation to the design) through 'back to front' feeding of sheets in the printing press. See 'Watermark—Inverted'.

Illustrations: V81, GB 'Penny Red', crown inverted; V82, GB, pair of KGV ½d. with crown missing.

Worn Plate. Descriptive of stamps printed from a plate in which the printing surface has deteriorated or worn.
Illustrations: V83, Venezuela; V84, Argentina, normal and pair from worn plate; V85, GB 'Penny Red'.

War Stamps. Issued under wartime conditions and so designated or inscribed.
Illustrations: W1, Oaxaca (Mexico); W2, Sonora (Mexico); W3, Baja California (Mexico); W4, Arequipa (Peru); W5, Spain; W6, Coruna (Spain); W7, Spain.

War Tax Stamps. Inscribed or overprinted 'WAR', 'WAR TAX', 'WAR STAMP' or in a foreign equivalent, issued for the purpose of raising funds in wartime, usually over and above the cost of postage.
Illustrations: W8, Malta; W9, Trinidad & Tobago; W10, North Borneo; W11, Ceylon; W12, Canada; W13, Spain; W14, Mozambique; W15, Spain.

Watermark. A design, device or pattern, i.e. a distinguishing mark, in paper, generally visible by transmitted light, formed by the dandy roll in the wet pulp stage of manufacture, in which the pressure of the attached 'bits' results in a thinning of the paper. The object—a security precaution against forgery. British stamps have ceased to be printed on watermarked paper.
Illustrations: W16, Denmark 'crown'; W17, Cochin 'parasol'; W18, Cape of Good Hope 'cabled anchor'.

All-over Watermark. A *single* device or pattern embracing the entire sheet of stamps. In some cases a proportion of the stamps may be left without watermark. Also 'sheet watermark'.
Illustrations: Rumania 'large arms' Watermark; W19, reduced-size illustration and, W20, part of watermark (which covers 25 stamps).

Gum Device. An imitation watermark on the gummed side of the stamps.
Illustration: W21, Czechoslovakia 1923, 'CSP' emblem on gum.

Impressed. An imitation watermark impressed on the stamp by die-stamping.
Illustration: W22, Switzerland 1862, impressed cross within oval.

Inverted. Certain stamps are normally issued with the watermark inverted, notably some of those issued in booklets by the British Post Office, due to the special arrangement of the printing plates or cylinders.
Illustration: W23, GB booklet pane.

W16

W17

W18

W19

W20

W21

W22

W23

W24

W25

W26

W27

W28

W29

W30

W31

W32

W33

Marginal. In some cases the watermarks extend to the sheet margins, in others the margins are clear. A marginal watermark is one specially inscribed or embodied in the sheet margin.
Illustration : W24, Turks Island 1882, 'Crown CA' watermark with 'CROWN AGENTS' in the margin ; full inscription— 'Crown Agents for the Colonies'.

Multiple. A watermark device repeated all over the sheet, so that each stamp may show several devices in whole or part.
Illustrations : W25, Persia, multiple 'arms' in circle ; W26, British Commonwealth 'Multiple Crown CA', and W27, 'Multiple Script CA'.

Overall Multiple. A network pattern covering all stamps in a sheet.
Illustration : W28, Thailand 'rectangles', also used in Panama (De La Rue paper stock).

Paper-maker's. A normal watermark incorporating the paper manufacturer's name or emblem, e.g. Maldive Islands 1933—'Harrison & Sons London'.

Printed. Imitation watermarks used to alleviate shortages or experimentally, as in Argentina (1922), Salvador (1935) and New Zealand.
Illustrations: W29, New Zealand 1925, 'NZ and Star' applied by litho-varnish.

Sideways. Watermarks may be found sideways in relation to the design of the stamp in cases where, due to the format of the stamp, it has been found more convenient to print them 'sideways-on'. The special arrangements for printing (British) roll stamps for sale in automatic vending machines also results in certain types of roll having stamps with sideways watermark.
Illustration: W30, Dominica 1d. 1921 with 'Mult. Script CA' watermark sideways.

Single. Watermark devices arranged so that each stamp bears a single device.
Illustrations: W31, British Commonwealth, single 'Crown CA'; W32, South Africa 'Springbok's Head'.

Stitch. Extraneous portions of a normal watermark, caused by stitches in the web—cloth or wire—on which the paper is manufactured.
Illustration : W33, USA 3 c. of 1870 with stitch watermark.

NOTE: The illustrations normally show the watermarks in reverse—as viewed through the backs of the stamps.

INDEX

First published as a part work in Gibbons *Stamp Monthly*
First published in book form 1973
Reprinted 1974
Second edition 1978
Reprinted 1979

ISBN 0 85259 895 5

Item No. 2740

Made and printed in Great Britain by Clarke, Doble and Brendon Limited, Plymouth and London